AmeriKKKa's Original Sin

A Collection of Essays on Racism and the Continuing Scourge of White Supremacy

K. GERALD TORRENCE

Copyright © 2025 by Gerald Torrence
All rights reserved.
ISBN: 979-8-89324-546-2

No part of this book may be reproduced, stored in a retrieval system, or transmitted in any form or by any means—electronic, mechanical, photocopying, recording, or otherwise—without prior written permission of the publisher, except for brief quotations used in reviews or articles.

The opinions expressed by the Author are not necessarily those held by the Publishers.

The information contained within this book is strictly for informational purposes. The material may include information, products, or services by third parties. As such, the Author and Publisher do not assume responsibility or liability for any third-party material or opinions. The publisher is not responsible for websites (or their content) that are not owned by the publisher. Readers are advised to do their own due diligence when it comes to making decisions.

Published by Franklin Publishers
Printed in the United States of America
For permissions, inquiries, or additional copies, contact:
Franklin Publishers
www.franklinpublishers.com

For my parents, Andrew and Marian

Table of Contents

Foreword	vi
Preface	ix
Acknowledgments	xii
THE TRUTH ABOUT RACISM	1
Donald Sterling and the Silent Majority	2
For the Love of Money: The Right to be Racist	5
Recognizing Racism	7
Tearing Down the Walls of Structural Racism	9
RACISM EXPOSED	13
The NFL's Latest Assault on Black Athletes	14
The New Plantation	18
Justice Department Discloses Rampant Racism	20
A Penal System That Punishes in Perpetuity	26
The Haves and the Have Nots	30
THE OBAMA EFFECT	34
The New Face of Western Imperialism	35
The Obama Backlash	38
The State of the American Negro	43
Obama's Refusal to Get It Right on Racism	48
The Movement Behind the Massacre	51
RACISM AND THE MEDIA	56
Death of Another Black Icon	57
Cable News' Attempts to Shape Public Opinion	59

Supreme Ignorance Is Not Confined to the Poor and Uneducated	62
Baltimore and Beyond … The Crisis Beneath the Crisis	65
BLACK LIVES MATTER	70
The Color of Justice	71
Uncle Toms in Blue	74
The (Not So) Curious Case of Sandra Bland	78
BACK TO BLACK	81
Back to Black	82
The New Black Power	88
References	92
Index	94
About the Author	95

Foreword

Dr. Love Henry Whelchel

Too many people talk about racial issues in America by employing vacuous platitudes and self-serving sound bites that show no evidence of serious study of the historical realities of racism and white supremacy. But how can we speak the truth about racism if we do not know the history of racial oppression? The prominent theologian and activist Jim Wallace has stated that telling the truth about race in America means acknowledging that racism is AmeriKKKa's original sin.

Any serious discussion or study of racial relationships in America will begin at the beginning or with the European Atlantic Slave Trade. It was the slave trade which initiated the most massive movement of human beings from one continent to another in world history. On one hand, the enslavement of Africans in the Americas enriched and empowered the European colonists as they sought their manifest destiny in the New World. On the other hand, chattel slavery meant social degradation, dehumanization, and marginalization for those enslaved.

All of the European nations involved in the slave trade and the enslavement of Africans were Christian nations. Slave traders and slave owners included practicing Roman Catholics, Baptists, Methodists, Presbyterians, Lutherans, Quakers, and Jews. They invoked their Judeo-Christian faith to ask God's blessings on their human trafficking and predatory exploitations. There were Christian chaplains aboard the slave ships, and the ships themselves were assigned Christian names such as Brotherhood, Charity, Gift of God, and Jesus. In short, the church officials were very much complicit along with the civil authorities in conducting and supporting one of the most monstrous crimes ever committed against a group of people in recorded history.

We may never know the exact number of Africans who were captured, herded into slave ships, and transported thousands of miles across the Atlantic Ocean to the Americas. It has been estimated that some 12 to 20 million made it across the Middle Passage from Africa to the Americas. But about one-third of those captured perished en route, and their bodies were thrown overboard to be devoured by sharks or to sink into watery graves.

Many would prefer to forget about the horrors and torments of American slavery. Graphic descriptions of the frequent beatings, rapes, and other abuses make us recoil in distress. The history of American chattel slavery is too painful to remember, but it is also much too dangerous to forget. For African Americans, reawakening our historical consciousness and obtaining a deep understanding of the painful realities of slavery that still inform and shape our social reality today are the keys to our political uprising, our economic renewal, and our spiritual liberation.

Alexis de Tocqueville, the famous French philosopher, gave voice to the future of racial problems in America more than 180 years ago. He correctly predicted that long after the Blacks were legally freed, they would still be ostracized and despised:

> There is a natural prejudice that prompts men to despise whoever has been their inferior long after he has become equal. In ancient times, there were slaves, but it was not based on skin color, and men could move from slavery to freedom without being recognized that they were once slaves. In America, after slavery has been abolished, God alone can obliterate the traces of the existence of slavery.

There is a direct correlation between the brutalities of American chattel slavery and the mindless violence, widespread destitution and squalor, high rates of unemployment, high rates of incarceration, and unhealthy lifestyles that we see running rampant in American society today. After the abolishment of legal enslavement, African Americans were still racially dominated as slavery was replaced by regimes of mass incarceration and the impediments of segregation, discrimination, and racial stereotypes. White people have continued to benefit from the presumption of white supremacy and the fact of white privilege in America.

We need to tell these truths if we wish to free ourselves from delusional falsehoods about our social reality. The work of K. Gerald Torrence is an impressive effort toward helping to bring us to just such a discourse. Such a discourse would also include an effort to tally up the tremendous debt still owed to those who were enslaved and their progeny. If America ever decides to have a meaningful and honest conversation about racism and white supremacy, then people will have to take seriously works of scholarship, righteous passion, and intellectual courage such as those provided by Mr. Torrence.

L.H. Whelchel, Jr.

Preface

K. Gerald Torrence

This project never started out as an attempt to write a book or even as an organized effort to compile a collection of essays on a single topic. The beginnings of this book started much more humbly and with no motivation other than to contemporaneously express my thoughts concerning some of the news events primarily affecting African Americans over the last two years. Gradually, these modest but heartfelt outpourings of thought and emotional reflection on current events took on a life of their own. It seemed, in retrospect, that every occurrence and every aspect of African American life was woven together with a common thread. This kneading is the constancy of racism and white supremacy that connects the earliest European contact with the African slave trade and the American Negro experience.

So, there was never any plan or thought given as to what would be the final product or whether these contemporaneous handwritten musings would be read or produced for anyone other than myself and a few friends as a way of obtaining feedback. Gradually, however, these inspired opinions on topics affecting African Americans began to take on a life of their own, and through the encouragement of Dr. L.H. Whelchel, I continued to write, fueled and inspired by various local, national, and international events of the last two years.

Although a child of the 60s with fresh memories of the assassination of Dr. Martin Luther King, Jr., the ensuing riots spawned by his death, and the emergence of the Black Power movement of the early 70s, I never considered myself a radical. This is despite the fact that I literally grew up on the college campuses of Tuskegee Institute and Tennessee State University, where my father, Dr. A.P. Torrence, served as provost and President, respectively. Although this privileged existence had a profound influence on my then still developing young psyche, it wasn't until later, at the age of 18 years, when I first heard Minister Louis Farrakhan deliver a thundering rebuke of white America's racist past on the weekly radio address "Muhammad Speaks" that I began to fully understand the historical two Americas—one black and one white. Even still, being aware of the message of the so-called "Black Muslims" and the rhetoric adopted by Malcolm X and Muhammad Ali, it never fully resonated at the time.

Unfortunately, like most African Americans, I went through most of life recognizing the disparities of being black in America and how it excluded me from certain aspects of white privilege. But I felt that it was just the way things were. The few but significant gains of the Civil Rights Era also seemed to inspire a complacency and false belief that, as Dr. King said, eventually, "we would get to the Promised Land" where we would "be judged not by skin color but by the content of our character."

It wasn't until I began to seriously study African, European, and American history with its racist and white supremacist underpinnings that I began to understand the opinions and writings of people like Frederick Douglass, Booker T. Washington, W.E.B. DuBois, Marcus Garvey, Carter G. Woodson, Howard Thurman, and others. Once I began to break the psychological chains of European miseducation and Euro-American revisionist history, the national and international incidents of the past 400 years began to make more sense. I then began to understand the real America through its racist past and present, which continues to give clarity to the experiences of the American Negro and the continuing struggle for an equality that still escapes us. It is only when we view local, national, and international events through the historical microscopic lens of racism and white supremacy that a true picture clearly emerges as to the depth of the ills of injustice, inequality, and lack of opportunities for the black man.

It was this process of historical study and inspiration that exposed the common thread that seemed to link every aspect of American culture and the 400-year odyssey of the Negro in America. The thread that was woven through the establishment of the colonies, through slavery, Reconstruction, Jim Crow, the Civil Rights Era, and the election of the first so-called "Black President" is the continuing presence of AmeriKKKa's original sin; it is the scourge of racism and white supremacy which is just as prevalent now as it was when the first slave ship landed in 1619 with its not so precious cargo of "twenty and odd Africans" aboard the Dutch warship in Point Comfort, Virginia.

Acknowledgments

K. Gerald Torrence

First and foremost, I would like to acknowledge my parents, Dr. Andrew P. Torrence and Mrs. Marian S. Torrence. They gave me the love and structure in my early life that allowed me to develop some good habits and an appreciation for learning. They also encouraged me to pursue my dreams, believing that I could achieve excellence if I did my very best. I must confess, this has not always been the case, but the seed was planted early, even if it took root late. My parents, who were both educators, also provided me with a nurturing environment and unlimited educational opportunities. My father (God rest his soul) firmly believed in the words of Booker T. Washington that "education was the best hope for the uplift of the Negro people." This belief was passed on to me as I have tried to emulate dad's life as an educator and a lifelong student of life and learning.

I must also acknowledge my aunt Rosalia Torrence who, as a retired English teacher, helped me to develop whatever writing skill that I had while a graduate and law student at the University of Arkansas at Little Rock.

Next, I have to give the utmost praise and acknowledgment to Dr. Love Henry Whelchel, my esteemed Professor at the Interdenominational Theological Center (ITC). It was Dr. Whelchel who stoked the fires of activism and black theological appreciation and liberation in me while I was a graduate student in his church history and African American church history classes. After all, it was Dr. Whelchel who gave me the name "The Truth Teller" and encouraged and recognized my potential as a writer and commentator on local, national, and world events.

Finally, I would like to thank Ms. Cindy Jones, my good friend, confidant, and the creative catalyst behind many of the images, concepts, and word processing required to launch this massive undertaking. Without her help, this book would not have been possible.

AmeriKKKa's Original Sin

True, This!
Beneath the rule of men entirely great
The pen is mightier than the sword.

Edward G. Bulwer-Lytton

THE TRUTH ABOUT RACISM

K. Gerald Torrence

Donald Sterling and the Silent Majority

Originally posted April 29, 2014

Why the righteous indignation over the racist diatribe of Los Angeles Clippers owner Donald Sterling? In a private conversation that was secretly recorded with his mistress, Sterling objects to her bringing black people to Clippers basketball games and reasons, "The world will think certain things if you're seen with black people, so you should not be seen with them in public." Is it not obvious to all that the deep stain of racism and prejudice runs deep in the culture and fabric of this Nation? How long will we continue to gloss over the fact that 500 years of systemized and institutional oppression based on skin color has—and still does—define this country?

The laws may have changed, but the attitudes that birthed and fostered white supremacy have not. Thank God that the comments of Donald Sterling have once again exposed the soft underbelly of American racist attitudes toward blacks. The veil has been lifted again on the façade of racial equality. With the intense media spotlight on the disturbing views of one of the NBA's billionaire owners, the hideous and ugly reality of intrinsic and ingrained hatred against African Americans is front and center—where it should be. It's past time that we dealt with the elephant in the room...this stinking albatross which hangs around the neck of America, masked by the perfume of political correctness and hypocrisy.

If things are ever to change, there first must be honesty in the discourse. This Nation has always been morally bankrupt and destitute in fairness and compassion for those who are still the wretched and despised great-grandsons and -granddaughters of former slaves. Make no mistake about it. Racism in this country is alive and well despite the election of President Barack Obama. What should have been a historic triumph over racism, his election has exacerbated the flames of latent—but still virulent—anti-black sentiment. To be honest, racism has never left; what's done and said in the dark eventually comes to light. Donald Sterling is no different from millions of other white men and women in this country. His views are the same, as are his sentiments. The only difference is that his private views have been made public. The invisible multitudes of Donald Sterling's whose world view and mouths drip with the venom of racial prejudice in private but wear the mask of public political correctness are legion. The elephant in the room has been exposed again. Good!

Now, let's have some honest dialogue about the ugly reality of pervasive racism in this country. Painful or not, we must stop acting like it doesn't exist and deal with it. What concerns me the most is that we have a Nation so racked by the guilt and shame of its racist past that it is afraid and embarrassed to acknowledge its racist present. Donald Sterling is not alone. He only stands alone because the millions of other Donald Sterlings are too cowardly to publicly admit the feelings and sentiments that they share privately. Until there is some honest recognition of the prevalence of racism in this country, we are powerless to address and change it.

Even the President chooses to tiptoe around the issue of racism for mainly political reasons. I'm sure he feels torn by divided loyalties based on his mixed genealogical heritage. He's both black and white. This is true even though he faces the reality of racism every day he serves as President. Many white people want and plot his failure simply because he is black (ask Rush Limbaugh, who was quoted as saying, "I hope he fails."). Many others hope he fails for the same reason—simply because he is black.

K. Gerald Torrence

This country was built, grew, and prospered on the principle of white superiority and black inferiority.

White or black, it's impossible to grow up in this country and not be tainted and shaped by the culture of racism and white superiority that has been the social and political reality for over 500 years. Consequently, it is sickening to hear the talking heads of white America express their righteous indignation at Donald Sterling when they, the silent majority, are indeed racist themselves. It is impossible to escape. Racism is too ingrained into the DNA of the United States. This country was built, grew, and prospered on the principle of white superiority and black inferiority.

Just like every promise and treaty that was broken with the Indians by the architects of the Constitution and their progeny, every promise of recompense and equity to the black man has been retracted and retreated from by the ruling white power structure. It's time for the truth to be told. How much longer will we allow the elephant in the room to be ignored? Just like the "emperor with no clothes," we are too afraid to acknowledge and voice the obvious. Until we embrace the ugly, entrenched stain of this country's racist past and present as a reality, we cannot begin to change it.

For the Love of Money: The Right to be Racist

Originally posted May 7, 2014

Although I do not agree with the racist views of Los Angeles Clippers owner Donald Sterling—who castigated his mistress for publicly fraternizing with black people—I wholeheartedly support his right to be a racist. In a country that was founded on the principles of freedom of speech and freedom of thought, the social and economic backlash against Sterling for expressing his private views is extremely troubling. It is yet another case of political correctness run amok.

How is it that thoughts expressed in a private setting, no matter how virulent and disturbing, can be the catalyst for the NBA equivalent of the death penalty? The NBA's unprecedented move to strip Donald Sterling of team ownership, ban him from the Clippers games, fine him 2.5 million dollars, and compel a forced sale of the team he's owned for 30 years—without a hearing—violates every principle of due process, equal protection, and freedom of speech.

What has our so-called democracy morphed into when the political heads of State can make subjective moral pronouncements, which serve to stifle the right to have differences of opinion? In today's America, the populace is afraid to voice any opinion that runs afoul of the politically correct view of the moment. At a time when the government increasingly infringes on the rights of the individual and privacy concerns are being eroded by the courts, these actions against the Clippers owner are all the more troubling.

Should it be the responsibility of government and special interest groups to establish the social and moral norms of a society? Or does democracy mean that all voices of expression have the right to be heard regardless of their identity with mainstream sentiment?

The NBA's move has set a dangerous precedent as we watch the black celebrities and social do-gooders line up behind the NBA's draconian coup of Sterling. Has it occurred to anyone what's really behind the NBA's swift and drastic action? Economics! It's naïve to think that NBA Commissioner Adam Silver and the rest of the NBA owners have suddenly got religion and, social, and moral epiphany. The NBA doesn't love black people, and neither does Adam Silver. Are we really to believe that Silver and the NBA's thirty white owners have all of a sudden become altruistic in the fight against racism—in embracing the cause of the African American? I think not. The billion-dollar conglomerate, which is the NBA, is simply posturing and jockeying to save its own financial interest. The economic viability of the NBA brand inures to the overwhelming benefit of its billionaire owners.

The NBA owners love money, and that's what Adam Silver's action was all about. With the risk of an NBA boycott by the Clippers players looming as a real possibility, Commissioner Silver—when faced with the potential loss of millions of dollars of playoff revenue and goodwill—took the only action deemed prudent. It was a financial decision, not a moral one. So let's not be fooled—the only color that matters in this sleight-of-hand, farcical move by the NBA is green.

Recognizing Racism

Originally posted May 15, 2014

Now that we've been publicly reminded that racism still exists, America must fight the temptation to continue to look the other way. Of course, it's much easier to label the racist comments of Los Angeles Clippers owner Donald Sterling an anomaly and shape the public perception of Sterling as simply a relic from the distant past. Those who live with the scourge of racism every day, however, know better. The intrinsic and insidious nature of institutionalized racism in this country is borne out by the fact that billionaire owner Sterling's views have been actualized in the corporate boardrooms of the NBA with acquiescence—if not acceptance—for over thirty years. It is only by accident or providence that Sterling's words were made public. Ironically, those familiar with Sterling have known his thoughts for decades.

This public perception of racism is what the NBA is now so desperately trying to erase. In a league that is dominated by African Americans, the threat and risk of a boycott by the players would be an economic Armageddon. This is why NBA Commissioner Adam Silver could say with a high degree of certainty that he had the backing of the NBA owners on the question of removing Sterling as an NBA owner. Of course, he does; this is not rocket science. Better to sacrifice one of its own than to risk the continued viability of the multi-billion-dollar industry, which is the NBA.

The problem with the honest acknowledgment and recognition of racism by the powerful entities capable of doing something about it is that an affirmative recognition requires an appropriate moral response. Once we honestly recognize racism as it is, we must then deal with the question that is begged by this acknowledgment: What is America willing to do to redress it? Once racism recognition has occurred, then society is morally compelled to redress it. This is precisely what America is afraid of … the moral and financial cost necessary to face and dismantle racism. No small order! It is much easier to pretend it doesn't exist or to delude the public with hyperbole about progress and disingenuous chatter about a post-racial society. The reality remains, however, that we are light-years away from this ever- elusive ideal. The critical question to be asked at this juncture is whether racial equality is something that the power brokers and the political pundits in this country really want. The overwhelming evidence so far suggests that the answer is a resounding "No"!

Unfortunately, America still lacks the willingness to face the reality of racism or the moral courage to change it.

Tearing Down the Walls of Structural Racism

Originally posted October 29, 2014

More than one hundred sixty years after the Civil War and the signing of the Emancipation Proclamation, the walls of structural and institutionalized racism continue to be erected. Rather than being torn down, these walls remain through the clever manipulation of voter registration laws, the creation of new barriers to equality through the criminal justice system, and the quasi-criminal institutions that control the social and societal norms of acceptable behavior in this country. Despite the passage of a number of Federal laws like the Civil Rights Acts of 1864 and 1964 aimed at state and local legally-sanctioned discrimination against blacks (commonly referred to as Jim Crow), the vestiges of separate but equal doctrines and outright monuments to white supremacy still exist.

Although abolished in principle by *Brown v. Board of Education*, the white power structures that run this country continue to find new and ingenious ways to maintain white supremacy and deny equal opportunity to the heirs and descendants of those who were undeniably responsible for creating much of the vast wealth of this country through slavery and free labor. Not only has America failed and refused to acknowledge this huge financial debt to the heirs of slavery, the rich and powerful white beneficiaries of the toil and sweat of generations of Negro slaves continue to reap the financial rewards of riches and vast wealth paid for with the blood and sweat of dead Negro slaves. This insult is added to the injury of additional modern-day laws and legislative enactments which further cripple the already limited prospects for African American advancement in a society still rife with the stains of centuries of unequal treatment based on race.

Recent legislative and legal attacks on black people, such as the War on Drugs, have resulted in a disproportionate number of black men incarcerated—close to 35% in 2014, although blacks make up less than 13% of the U.S. population.[1] The other war on "dead-beat dads" masquerades as state and federal policy to hold fathers accountable but, in reality, results in the further marginalization and incarceration of black men. The U.S. Constitution specifically forbids the incarceration of U.S. citizens for a debt, yet millions of black fathers face incarceration and loss of basic liberties. Furthermore, tens of thousands of black males within the workforce are plucked out of gainful employment after being arrested—sometimes on the job—for child support delinquency. This type of moronic logic not only further reduces the number of gainfully employed black males but also feeds and swells the prison industrial complex, further depleting African American participation in the social structures of family and the pursuit of liberty and happiness. After release from prison and jails, the African American male is almost guaranteed no job—or, at best, a menial one that fails to provide enough income to sustain his family or freedom— and no chance to avoid the revolving door of recidivism and perpetual poverty.

Incarcerated blacks often do not have the basic resources to obtain bond, thereby insuring that they remain imprisoned for months at a time, often for petty and minor offenses. This form of legalized oppression geometrically multiplies the incidence of single black mothers raising children with no male support. Then, once released from prison after having paid their debt to society, as convicted felons, they are forever penalized and denied full citizenship by the stigma and the loss of rights resulting from a criminal record. It's a vicious and morally indefensible cycle.

Surely, the learned white men of the U.S. Senate and House of Representatives are smart enough to realize the catastrophic and genocidal effects of the legislative policies and legal enactments that they pass on black men. Assuming arguendo that they do not, then they are unfit to be in office. If we correctly presume the former, then it follows that their actions and intentions are consistent with the results— a legal and social system that disparately impacts and punishes black Americans, irrespective of presumed constitutional protections and basic principles of justice and equality. The systemic problems of structural racism and white supremacy are multi-faceted and complex, but we can't continue to look the other way or be content with the snail's pace of incremental progress and the clever but oppressive tactics of addition by subtraction. The budgets for food stamps, unemployment insurance, aid for families with dependent children, social security, reduced school lunches, public education, and a myriad of other programs to help the poor are slashed or eliminated by Presidents and other elected officials. Yet the Federal government spends trillions on death and destruction abroad through its war machine, and the top 1% of Americans get richer while everybody else continues to lose financial ground.

We must lift our voices and our ballots to demand the only remedy for 500 years of systemic racial and financial inequality in this country.

The values and priorities of this country are reflected by these disparities. Despite potent and consistent propagandist rhetoric that suggests things are okay, the disparate realities for black and brown people are in stark contrast. When the white man catches a cold, the black man gets the flu. We can't continue to wait on white folk to give us equality—this they will never do willingly. We must lift our voices and our ballots to demand the only remedy for 500 years of systemic racial and financial inequality in this country.

K. Gerald Torrence

Reparations Now! It is only through the payment of the debt owed to African Americans, representing trillions of dollars in economic benefit to this country from centuries of slave labor by our ancestors, that black people can hope to attain any level of economic and legal equality in this country. Otherwise, the vast ocean of distance between white wealth and black is a distance that will never be closed. America was built on the backs of blacks, and they haven't been paid yet.

They had for more than a century before been regarded as beings of an inferior order and altogether unfit to associate with the white race, either in social or political relations; and so far inferior that they had no rights which the white man was bound to respect; and that the Negro might justly and lawfully be reduced to slavery for his benefit.

Chief Justice Roger B. Taney
March 1857
The Dred Scott Decision

RACISM EXPOSED

K. Gerald Torrence

The NFL's Latest Assault on Black Athletes

Originally posted November 20, 2014

The NFL's latest disciplinary action against Minnesota Vikings star running back Adrian Peterson smacks of institutional and structural racism. Plain and simple, it is a continuing attack on the African American male by the establishment in an attempt to further emasculate and marginalize the black male's position as a patriarch of African American families.

These attacks on the black male are nothing new. They date back to the inception of the transatlantic slave trade, in which black males were systematically brutalized and victimized for the purpose of subjugating the race. White slaveholders realized that if the black male could be reduced to a sniveling, shuffling, head-scratching character, then the entire race of African Americans could be held in check. To accomplish this societal, political, and cultural result, a number of insidious but ingenious plans were implemented that would have the effect of reducing the black male's standing in the familial structure and upsetting any type of hierarchical leadership or perceived authority that might normally be associated with the head of family.

Peterson, initially charged with felony child abuse after whipping his four-year-old boy with a switch, plead no contest recently to a misdemeanor, thereby concluding the criminal case pursuant to compliance with community/public service announcements against domestic violence. While the criminal case played out, Peterson was serving an eight-game suspension from the NFL with pay under a "Commissioner's exception." After applying for reinstatement following the conclusion of the criminal matter, NFL Commissioner Roger Goodell refused Peterson's reinstatement request and declared the player ineligible for the remainder of the season, returning no earlier than April 15, 2015. In a letter, Goodell further stated that the switch Peterson used was "the functional equivalent of a weapon" and that Peterson's return to the NFL would depend on Peterson's actions after finding that the player showed "no meaningful remorse." With Peterson's return contingent on his "understanding the nature of his transgressions," i.e., learning his lesson, this treatment violates the spirit of the legal concept of double jeopardy, which dictates that a man cannot be tried or punished twice for the same offense. All of this for an act of child discipline, which for decades has been accepted as part of black culture. Even the *Holy Bible* says, "…those who love them [children] are diligent to discipline them" (Proverbs 13:24, New Revised Standard Version).

What started as a movement against spanking in the schools moved into the homes of black people …

Here we have just the latest instance of white folk dictating cultural norms for black families to the detriment of African Americans. This attack on the cultural norms of discipline in black families began in the 1960s with the advent of desegregation. Prior to integration, black children were taught, reared, and disciplined without interference from white folks. During these pre-integration years, black kids such as myself were the models of decorum and self-control. I believe a main ingredient in the rise of pre-integration African Americans was the rule of corporal punishment at home and in schools. After integration, corporal punishment was disallowed in public schools because white folk didn't want black teachers applying physical discipline to white kids. Consequently, what started as a movement against spanking in the schools moved into the homes of black people, with departments of child and social services becoming the arbiters of what constituted proper discipline of black kids.

This intrusion by white folks into the rearing of black children correlates with the endemic rise of black youth being funneled into the pipeline of the American industrial prison complex and the criminal justice system. Although blacks make up a mere 13% of the U.S. population, in 2014, we represent 35% of the inmates in American jails and prisons.[2] Is this huge disparity because of blacks' innate propensity to crime? I think not! The answer, to be sure, is multifaceted, but undoubtedly, part of the problem is the inability of black families to discipline their children in the time-honored and culturally accepted norm of corporal punishment. Today, black kids grow up in environments where there is a lack of discipline and respect for authority in the home and the schools. The result is the disparate numbers of black kids dropping out of school and being dropped into the increasingly privatized corporate prison system, which rewards private investors based on the number of prison beds that are occupied.

Let us not be fooled by the Uncle Tom, handkerchief-head, sell-out Negroes who mouth whatever is convenient or palatable ...

As for Adrian Peterson, I applaud him. I applaud him for the courage to stare down Roger Goodell and the lynch mob mentality of the American media, which has declared outright war on the black male, as illustrated in the recent cases of Ray Rice, Adrian Peterson, and others. To Peterson's credit, he has stood up and said that he would "not eliminate whipping his kids." Kudos to you, Mr. Peterson! Some things are more important than football and the fickle perceptions of public opinion endorsed by white America.

Let us not be fooled by the Uncle Tom, handkerchief-head, sellout Negroes who mouth whatever is convenient or palatable through the oppressive cable news network conglomerates. These shameless Negroes will curse their own mothers just for a chance to sit at the table with the white news media, thereby gaining a distorted sense of credibility—and for a few pieces of silver!

K. Gerald Torrence

The New Plantation

Originally posted December 4, 2014

When I see major college football powerhouses like Alabama, FSU, and Auburn, I see the plantations that my forefathers slaved on all over again. Big time college athletics has become the latest reincarnation of chattel slavery: white men exploiting the skill and free labor of strong black bodies to build wealth and power for the edification and glorification of white institutions.

Take a look at any top five football team, or top twenty-five for that matter; the only things white are the multi-millionaire coaches and the referees. This money grab takes place at the top while impoverished black players have to hustle and steal for the pocket change necessary for dignity and survival. Across the collegiate football landscape, it appears that a large majority of the skill players are black, save for a token white boy here and there just for the sake of reverse "diversity." This overwhelming African American presence is a far cry from 50 years ago when white schools didn't want the black athlete or the black student. Remember 1963, when then-Governor George Wallace stood on the steps of the University of Alabama, blocking the entrance of two African American students. In the now immortalized words of the staunch segregationist, he defiantly threw down the gauntlet at the seat of perceived tyranny and declared, "Segregation today, segregation tomorrow, and segregation forever."

My, how things have changed! But how much have things really changed? I submit that the only difference between 1964 and 2014 is that they took the signs down that said "colored" and "whites only."

Overall, the racist attitudes of whites toward what Supreme Court Justice Taney called "that unfortunate class of beings that is enslaved for his own good" still remain strong. Ask Donald Sterling. The NBA and the NFL owners all share the same racist heritage and legacy. Sterling was not an anomaly. Professional sports teams are owned by wealthy white billionaires whose avocation is to make money off the skill and athletic ability of the black male. Do they respect the black athlete? No. Look no further than the cases of Ray Rice and Adrian Peterson. Roger Goodell essentially did everything but call them n s, especially after the winds of public opinion demanded a pound of black flesh for alleged offenses that white men have committed for years with impunity.

I long for the days when we had black football powerhouses like Tennessee State, Grambling, and Southern University. White professional scouts would camp out at black schools for the chance to draft the next Claude Humphrey, Richard Dent, or "Jefferson Street" Joe Gilliam. Now, only the third- and fourth-tier black athletes attend black colleges, and consequently, black collegiate athletics are only a shell of what once was a proud and storied legacy. The beneficiaries of this mass exodus of blue chip black athletes has been the traditionally segregated white schools, which were built and financed by slave labor. How ironic is it that these wealthy institutions continue to prosper on the backs of blacks while our beloved Historically Black Colleges and Universities (HBCUs), which educated and trained us when the white schools would not, are struggling to maintain students and keep the doors open. It's a sad commentary.

Just imagine what would happen if our prized athletes were to return to our HBCUs and the mass flood of black students flocking to the semi-segregated white universities were to come home? The fortunes and careers of our black athletes would still skyrocket. It's talent that drives the NFL. The financial boon in revenue and income from athletics, however, would start to benefit black people and black institutions instead of continuing to increase the wealth and supremacy of the racist institutions that keep us oppressed.

K. Gerald Torrence

Justice Department Discloses Rampant Racism

Originally posted April 15, 2015

The long-awaited findings of the U.S. Justice Department investigation into the Ferguson, Missouri Police Department contained no new news for African Americans. The Department of Justice report detailing the pervasive, systemic, and structural forms of racism in the police department and city government comes as no surprise to those who live out this reality every day. The African American victims of these and other oppressive, racist regimes in state and local governments across this nation didn't need the Justice Department confirmation of what we already know. America and its cities and municipalities are rife with racism.

The Justice Department's finding that the Ferguson police department and city's municipal court engaged in a "pattern and practice" of discrimination against African Americans, targeting them disproportionately for traffic stops, use of force, and jail sentences, is at least partial vindication for the thousands of Ferguson-area residents and supporters who marched and protested after the murder of unarmed teenager Michael Brown.

As reported and reviewed by CNN, among the findings from 2012 to 2014:

- 85% of people subject to vehicle stops by Ferguson police were African Americans

- 90% of those who received citations were black
- 93% of people arrested were black.

This occurred while 67% of the Ferguson population is black.³

In 88% of the cases in which Ferguson police reported using force, it was against African Americans. During this period, 2012-2014, black drivers were twice as likely as white drivers to be searched during traffic stops but 23% less likely to be found in possession of contraband. Additionally, blacks were disproportionately more likely to be cited for minor infractions: 95% of tickets for "manner of walking in roadway," essentially jaywalking, were against African Americans. Also, 94% of all "failure to comply" charges were filed against black people. African Americans were also 68% less likely to have their cases dismissed by a Ferguson municipal judge and overwhelmingly more likely to be arrested during traffic stops solely for an outstanding warrant by the Ferguson courts.⁴

It's no wonder why Americas' jail cells over- represent African Americans at a rate of 35%, even though we represent less than 13% of the general population.

The illumination of these realities, while welcome, is not dispositive of the long-standing practice of state and local governments balancing their financial books on the backs of blacks who are many times mired in poverty and the least able to afford these unlawful and unconstitutional violations; these violations are perpetrated under the guise of law and order and the public safety needs of the community. These oppressive and unconstitutional violations against African Americans are not isolated in their occurrences. Across this country, local, municipal, and state courthouses are full of black people in disproportionate numbers as compared to whites. Take a look at any urban municipal courthouse across America, and it is as if blacks are the only ones committing traffic violations or other crimes. Consequently, it's no wonder why America's jail cells over- represent African Americans at a rate of 35% in 2014,[5] even though we represent less than 13% of the general population.

The Ferguson case is eerily reminiscent of the case of Donald Sterling, the billionaire former owner of the Los Angeles Clippers NBA franchise, whose racist comments ignited a social and political firestorm resulting in a forced sale of the team. We've seen this movie before! The cable news networks and political pundits will use their enormous social and political influence to portray the toxic racist environment in the Ferguson police department and city government as an isolated incident. This only serves to preserve a culture of systemic racism and white supremacy while prescribing a quick fix with a few token gestures of "change," which do not address the systemic and pervasive nature of racism in every facet of American culture. The system is allowed then to continue unabated while the root causes of the problem remain unchecked. It is akin to treating the symptoms of a disease without addressing the cause. It's impossible to provide an effective cure without a proper diagnosis. No wonder this country fails to make any real progress toward eradicating racial discrimination in this country.

Those who continue to profit from the culture of white supremacy see the dismantling of the centuries-old system as a threat to their monopoly on wealth and power. Look at the makeup of the U.S. House and Senate. It's a sea of white men and white women with a darkie thrown in here or there for the sake of appearances. More than 50 years after the Civil Rights Act of 1964, the Negro is still mired in a system of white supremacy which leaves them marginalized and oppressed. This culture of white dominance and Black subjugation filters down from the executive office through the halls of congress to state and local governments, tainting courts, administrative offices, and the officials and staff that run them.

If there ever is to be real change in the cultural, structural, and endemic racial inequality in America, we must first acknowledge and recognize a society that, in many ways, is the same as it was before the Emancipation Proclamation. Justice Taney voiced the true feelings of white America in the *Dred Scott v. Sandford* decision which denied the Negro status as a citizen: "the Negro has no rights which the white man is bound to respect." This pronouncement by the highest court in the land undergirds the cultural and social fabric of America today, just as it did over 150 years ago when Taney purported to speak for all civilized people of the world when he called the Negro "an unfortunate race that is enslaved for his own good." White America didn't view the Negro as an equal then, and they don't view us as equals now. Until there is a fundamental change of this reality, the more things change, the more they will remain the same.

Now that the curtain has been pulled back and the systemic oppression and systematic targeting of Blacks has been exposed in Ferguson, what is the remedy? A consent decree between the city of Ferguson and the Justice Department are only a start. Any true and meaningful remedy must address and redress the economic, social, and psychological injuries to the tens of thousands of African Americans in Ferguson who were victimized by its racist and unjust system. Liberty and freedom was lost due to systemic and discriminatory incarceration; homes and living quarters were lost due to inability to make mortgage and car payments. Monies earmarked for food and shelter were siphoned from family budgets to fund the corrupt city and local governments, which in turn perpetuated the cycle of predatory and systemic oppression of Black people. This form of economic and cultural genocide was not done to minorities, i.e., white women, Hispanics, gays, and lesbians, or any other multitude of individuals under America's new smorgasbord of stated and unstated protected classes. It was done to Black people! America has apparently forgotten and removed the Negro from its consciousness as the original minority in this country.

There must be a nationwide review of policies and practices ... to root out and remedy these continuing constitutional abuses.

Ferguson is only the tip of the iceberg. These types of racist policies and structures in police departments, courts, and state and local governments are rampant throughout this country. Every municipality is guilty and, therefore, culpable and responsible for the solution. Justice demands that the Federal Government not end its investigation at Ferguson but conduct a state by state, city by city, municipality by municipality audit of policies and practices and expose the true picture of America. The ugly truth is that the United States of America is a country rife with racism and injustice while hiding behind the façade of fairness, human rights, and democratic values. How dare America condemn Communist, Socialist, and autocratic regimes when it continues to maintain its 400-year legacy of systemic and structural deprivation of rights and equality to the black man? There must be a nationwide review of policies and practices of Federal, municipal, state, and local governments to root out and remedy these continuing constitutional abuses.

Now that we've documented the problem to the extent that the racist practices cannot be rationalized or theorized beyond the cold, hard facts, it's time to fashion a remedy. Call it reparations, or call it a remedy. You can call the legal and economic mechanism used to address and redress these continuing harms to African Americans, whatever is most palatable to the power brokers in the halls of Congress and the Executive Branch. (Just don't call it a hand out. This money is owed!) But whatever you call the remedy, it must be comprehensive, and it must not only address the problem and the solution but also the victims and the financial harm that they have suffered. Economic redress for the systemic racist policies and practices of state and local governments must be a part of any solution or comprehensive remedy. No matter what the cost, no matter how long and laborious the process, if America is serious about correcting a system of governance that has engaged in patterns and practices of discrimination deeply rooted in the fiber and fabric of this nation, it must be done, and it must be done now.

AmeriKKKa's Original Sin

If America can spend a billion dollars a day to finance imperialist military interventions across the globe, it can afford to redress the continuing civil, constitutional, and human rights violations of its most marginalized and historically oppressed people: African American citizens.

K. Gerald Torrence

A Penal System That Punishes in Perpetuity

Originally posted May 29, 2015

Logic and common sense would seem to dictate that after a man serves time in prison and has repaid his debt to society, he should be allowed to re-enter the free world with all the rights and privileges appertaining thereto. This right to re-enter society and choose a new path of honest and lawful living, in fact, should be encouraged and even enabled with the help of government funds and programs. This is the only sensible course of action if a society wants a reformed and useful citizen returning to the streets of America, as opposed to the all too common revolving door of criminality in this country that tends to perpetuate an underclass of black and brown people with no hope for a different or better way of life. The unfortunate reality is that the exact opposite is true. When convicted felons are re-introduced in society, they are virtual pariahs with reduced rights and limited options for gainful legal employment that allows for a chance at the American dream.

Under the current United States penal system, a nominal term of confinement often results in a virtual life sentence, where ex-offenders are forever tied to their past as well as a future that offers fewer opportunities to break from it. The continuing cycle of poverty, crime, and institutionalization is fueled by government policy and practice that severely restricts the traditional economic options available to the convicted felon.

As reported by *The Wall Street Journal*, in the majority of states, a convicted drug felon is unable to "vote, teach preschool, foster a child, operate a race track, cut hair, sit on a jury, provide hospice care, protect wild game, distribute bingo supplies, deal livestock, broker real estate, or obtain a license to become a heating, ventilation and air conditioning technician."[6] These "civil sanctions," triggered by a criminal conviction, are the result of thousands of federal and state legal enactments over the past forty years which forever deny a convicted felon of living life as a normal citizen. Coincidentally, over the same four decades, according to *WSJ*, "the U.S. prison population has grown from fewer than 400,000 inmates to about 1.5 million"[7] and counting. Fueled by drug laws that disproportionately target and impact African Americans and the growth industry of "privatized" for-profit prison systems, there seems to be no end in sight to the escalation of the American industrialized prison complex.

Hope and equality ... which after 400 years, continue to elude us despite the myriad of constitutional amendments ...

It's almost as if some Oz-like character intent on perpetuating the culture of white supremacy and Negro oppression decrees from behind the veiled curtain of hypocrisy and political correctness, "I know how to solve the Negro problem: we'll create within the race a substantial underclass which will never be able to rise from the ashes of their own poverty, hopelessness, and lack of opportunity." This same scenario is played out in the Biblical text. In Exodus 1:10, the new king of Egypt observes that the Israelites are becoming more numerous and declares, "Come let us deal shrewdly with them, or they will increase and in the event of war join our enemies and fight against us." A different context, but the perceived problem and the proposed solution are analogous to modern times. This secret agenda is carried out and sells a false dream of hope and equality to African Americans; which, after 400 years of servitude and second class citizenship, continues to elude us despite the myriad of constitutional amendments and passage of civil and voting rights acts designed to address legalized discrimination.

This hypothetical analogy is applicable because blacks have become the face of the American criminal justice system. Although we represent less than 13% of the population, we are 35% of all state and federal prisoners in 2014.[8] There is something terribly wrong with this picture! Although some might scoff at this notion of a conspiracy to continue the subjugation of the black race through American courts, jails, law enforcement, and other institutions, the discriminatory and disparate impact is undeniable. When the lily-white Federal and State legislators pass arcane and liberty-divesting laws that overwhelmingly impact African Americans, what color is the face of those who they see these laws affecting? Certainly not people who look like them. There is no way intelligent people can pass laws which perpetuate an underclass of society's dredges and discardibles by accident. The face of the criminal, the face of the undesirable, and the face of the boogeyman in America has always been painted black. Intentionally!

I believe it more than coincidence that the avalanche of civil sanctions that accompany criminal convictions just so happens to disparately impact black people.

By limiting the job prospects of so many African American past offenders, the federal and state governments effectively ensure that prison populations will continue to be revolving doors of hopelessness, fed by a system that not only incarcerates but also castigates and eliminates legitimate economic opportunity for the life of the released former inmate. This perpetual punishment, though not physical, is a life sentence that robs the individual, their families, and communities of any reasonable chance of uplift for generations to come. It also insures that there will be an ever-present and ever-increasing pool of minority inmates to continue to maximize the profits for white investors and subsidize kickbacks to crooked judges, prosecutors, state attorneys, and law enforcement officials. It's all a big racket, with the only winners being the white institutions and their establishment types that profit from them. Such a diabolical scheme is the thing of which conspiracy theories are made. Unfortunately, truth often proves itself to be stranger and more unbelievable than fiction. I believe it more than coincidence that the avalanche of civil sanctions that accompany criminal convictions just so happens to disparately impact black people.

A brief look at America's past provides all of the precedent needed to connect the dots and draw solid conclusions. United States history is replete with organized attempts by politicians and elected officials to "stack the deck" in favor of the white majority. When viewed through the lens of history, such dastardly and blatantly discriminatory acts, such as a plan to perpetuate African American incarceration and exacerbate systemic social and economic inequality, seem not only plausible but likely. White folk would be hard pressed to devise a more effective plan of subjugating a race and ensuring its relegation to the revolving doors of criminality and the choices that lead to lives of hopelessness, institutionalization, and death. The current American penal system accomplishes this in spades.

K. Gerald Torrence

The Haves and the Have Nots

Originally posted November 4, 2015

Over the past forty years, the United States has increasingly become a country of the haves and the have-nots. This growing inequality of wealth and income threatens to undermine the very fabric of American life. As the middle class disappears, the so-called "American Dream" is becoming unreachable even for those working-class whites accustomed to being the perceived rightful beneficiaries of America's wealth and vast resources. At the other end of the spectrum, America's traditionally despised and neglected populace, the African Americans, falls deeper and deeper into the self-perpetuating cycle of poverty and hopelessness that has decimated the black community. This decimation is evidenced by the mass incarceration of black males and the rising tide of violence and lawlessness in black neighborhoods, oftentimes aimed at other blacks who become intended and sometimes unintended victims.

Interestingly enough, the spiraling poverty and hopelessness of African Americans should come as a surprise to no one. In fact, this ever worsening condition of blacks in America was predicted and warned against by officials in the highest levels of government. In July 1967, President Lyndon Johnson formed an 11-member advisory commission informally known as the "Kerner Report" to study civil disorder and to explain the riots that plagued American cities each summer since 1964. The Commission's report concluded that the nation was "moving toward two societies, one black, and one white—separate and unequal." Unless the conditions were remedied, the Commission warned, the country faced a "system of apartheid in its major cities." The "Kerner

Report" went on to deliver an indictment of "white society" for isolating and neglecting African Americans and urged legislation to promote integration and to enrich slums primarily through job creation, job training programs, and decent housing. President Johnson, however, rejected the recommendations.

In 1998, thirty years after the issuance of the Report, former Senator Fred Harris co-authored a study that found the racial divide had grown in the ensuing years with inner city unemployment at crisis levels. Opposing voices, however, argued that the Commission's dire predictions failed to materialize due to a marked increase in the number of African Americans living in the suburbs. This false rhetoric has served to obscure the facts and drown out the few voices of truth and reason that have been, in essence, "crying in the wilderness."

> *"The Negro community has been forced into a matriarchal structure which ... imposes a crushing burden on the Negro male ... "*

Another report (headed by former Senator and advisor to President Nixon, Daniel Patrick Moynihan), called "The Negro Family: The Case for National Action," also sounded the alarm to the growing inequality and disparity of opportunity for African Americans. As described in *The Atlantic*, "the federal government was underestimating the damage done to black families by three centuries of unimaginable mistreatment as well as a racist virus in the American blood stream which would continue to plague blacks in the future."[9] The article continues with an excerpt from the Moynihan report which read, "in essence, the Negro community has been forced into a matriarchal structure which, because it is so out of line with the rest of the American society, seriously retards the progress of the group as a whole and imposes a crushing burden on the Negro male, and in consequence, on a great many Negro women as well."[10]

Approximately 72% of all black babies are born out of wedlock. This fact alone triggers a host of catastrophic ripple effects in and around black communities.[11] This disintegration of traditional families leaves young, school-aged black children to be raised by the streets under the influence of rap music, reality TV, and the overwhelming impact of social media. Interestingly and alarmingly, this figure of black unwed mothers was only 24% in 1965 when Moynihan produced "The Negro Family" report. The number of black babies born out of wedlock has tripled since then and continues to spiral out of control with no end in sight.

If we, as black people, continue to do nothing to force change, then change will not occur.

Although the problems of our communities have long ago reached epidemic proportions, it seems that no one seems to care. Those African Americans fortunate enough to have escaped the slums and ghettos of modern day inner city life have mostly turned a blind eye and a deaf ear to the acute problems of poverty and under privilege affecting the majority of blacks in this country. We have taken the attitude of extreme "me-ism": if it doesn't affect me, then I'm not worried about it. I'm reminded of the words of Dr. Martin Luther King, Jr., however, when he said, as I paraphrase: Injustice and inequality anywhere affects justice and equality everywhere. My question is this: If we, the few African American success stories, survive or thrive while the masses of our people and communities are ravaged by poverty and hopelessness, have we really succeeded? If we, as black people, don't exercise some care and compassion for our own people, how can we expect the white man to care? Power only responds or concedes to force that is equal to or greater than it. If we, as black people, continue to do nothing to force change, then change will not occur.

The pipe dream that was "President Obama the Savior" should have taught us this valuable lesson. Even President Obama was able to ignore the plight and suffering of his own people's condition as a result of not being held accountable to us by us. President Obama sailed into office with the strength of the black vote in both elections yet has done nothing to address the concerns of black voters. Although black folk believed in the dream and the hype of the first black President, we failed to understand that Obama, unfortunately, above all else, is a politician. He is a politician who played on the emotions and dreams of the voting populace to achieve the objective of winning an election. What happens after the election depends on the concessions gained by the special interests or voting blocks that were demanded and secured before the elections took place.

The wealthy white gay rights lobby proved this point. Remember, President Obama was initially against gay marriage. He changed his course and opinion on the issue mid-stream after extreme political and financial pressure by the powerful white gay rights lobby, which held the keys to President Obama's re-election. Consequently, President Obama had a "come to Jesus" moment and began to view gay marriage rights as human rights. Was Obama's change of heart political astuteness or political correctness, all in the name of so called "equality"? You decide!

In the end, President Obama has now become known as the nation's first "Gay President," having ushered in the era of a rainbow-colored White House and the LGBTQ community as a protected class. Until black folk stop automatically voting for Democrats or other candidates because they are black without demanding accountability and instead forcing them to earn our vote, the cycle of politics as usual and the inconsequence of black poverty, inequality, and hopelessness will continue unabated.

In the history of this country, there has never been a President so vilified, insulted, and undermined by congressmen through action and inaction which belie their claims of legitimate policy differences.

K. Gerald Torrence
April 2015
"Obama's Refusal to Get It Right On Racism"

THE OBAMA EFFECT

The New Face of Western Imperialism

Originally posted September 24, 2014

As the United States again rallies European support (under the guise of NATO) for another military foray into the Middle East in the name of freedom and democracy, the face of Western Imperialism and colonialism has changed. The players, the United States, Great Britain, France, and Germany, remain the same, but the face of this long- standing European alliance is now black. Barack Hussein Obama, the 42nd president of the United States, has willingly or unwittingly assumed the leadership mantle of Western Imperialism. This has taken place despite the fact that he was elected and re-elected President on an anti-war platform. After less than a year in office, Obama was even awarded the Nobel Peace Prize. How ironic that now, six years into his presidency, he has conducted more drone strikes than President George W. Bush and aided and abetted in the massacre of hundreds of innocent Palestinian women and children through overt and covert U.S. financial and military support of Israel. It's no secret that many of the weapons used by the Israeli armed forces against the Palestinian homeland are made in the U.S. and are paid for with U.S. military aid to Israel. This massacre was waged and justified by the Israeli government in spite of the strong public outcry denouncing the savage slaughter of the Palestinians in its most recent 60-day bombing onslaught.

Even more ironic is the fact that a black man is now poised to perpetuate the slaughter and destruction of thousands more people of color in the name of liberation, freedom, and democracy. The U.S. killed over 200,000 Iraqis in the Gulf Wars under President Bush

Senior and Junior, which were both wars of questionable necessity, to say the least. The stated mission of the second Gulf War was to destroy weapons of mass destruction that, as it turned out, didn't exist. The U.S. mission was then amended to be for "the liberation of the Iraqi people." Trillions of dollars and hundreds of thousands of lives later, Iraq, Libya, and Syria have devolved into the hot-beds of Islamic extremism that have given rise to the civil wars and sectarian violence that now engulf the Middle East.

Make no mistake, the misguided U.S. policies of military conquest and covert operations to foster regime change and the placement of Western-backed puppet governments in the Middle East is the catalyst for the meteoric rise of militant groups like ISIS and al- Shabab. With every Iraqi, Syrian, Palestinian, and African we and our so-called allies kill in the name of the "war on terror," we spawn a thousand more virulent enemies of the West. As we have seen, these new and growing enemies of the West are willing to exact vengeance by any means necessary, including suicide bombers and beheadings. How long will this military assault on people of color continue before right-thinking people have the consciousness and courage to call it what it is— genocide! We've seen this example played out in history before. It only takes a quick glance at history to understand that the path America is taking is nothing new. Go back to the Roman Empire and its fall, and then compare the similarities. The analogies are striking: burdensome taxes on the middle and lower class; a widening and unconscionable gap between rich and poor, where an increasing majority of citizens fall into the categories of poverty or near-poverty. Just like ancient Rome, we have tax burdens that fall disproportionately on the poor while the rich escape taxes through an unfair system that rewards the wealthy through disparate tax obligations and loopholes; military opportunism, and occupation far beyond our borders under the guise of liberation and democracy. The writing is on the wall. The same fate that befell Rome awaits the United States of America.

> *The cruelest irony of all is that a black face is being used to perpetuate the genocide taking place ...*

As racial disparities and discrimination at home illuminate the continuing oppression of African Americans through the killing of unarmed black men in New York and Ferguson, Missouri, the centuries-old marginalization and subjugation of people of color takes on a new and urgent relevance. These most recent blatant and latent forms of discrimination against African Americans should once and for all shatter the charade of a post-racial society being promulgated by white Americans. As America's military war machine amps up for another war under the pretext of humanitarian aid and militarized police forces across the nation turn their weapons of war on unarmed black and brown civilians, what's next?

The cruelest irony of all is that a black face is being used to perpetuate the genocide taking place in American cities like Ferguson and others and all across the Middle East and Africa. The comparisons are striking. The new face of Western Imperialism is now black.

K. Gerald Torrence

The Obama Backlash

Originally posted January 11, 2015

The election of Barack Hussein Obama as the first African American President was hailed by most as a watershed moment in the centuries-old struggle for racial equality in America. This miraculous achievement was, in the minds of many, proof positive that we had overcome the barriers of endemic and systemic racism in this country. While Mr. Obama's election indeed was an accomplishment that most thought would never come, it by no means has signaled an end to the structural and systemic racism that is part and parcel of the DNA of the United States of America. In fact, what was widely viewed as a victory for black progress has, in reality, mobilized the forces of white supremacy like no other event in this nation's history since the debacle of Reconstruction after the Civil War. We've been down this road before. There is an historical precedent for white backlash against black progress, real or imagined.

Mr. Obama's election, like Reconstruction, began as a moment of great promise in tearing down the walls of inequality and leveling the playing field between blacks and whites in this country. In reality, it did nothing more than stir the pot of anti-black sentiment. This backlash against black progress, then and now, has a similar origin. It is grounded in the principle of white supremacy. After President Abraham Lincoln signed the Emancipation Proclamation, the question of "What to do with the Negro?" was paramount in the minds and hearts of the leaders of this nation.

The answer to that question was influenced in part by the acknowledgment that the Negro had contributed mightily to the victory of the North over the South and the preservation of the Union. Over 200,000 black troops fought valiantly for the Union army to overcome what started off as a losing cause against an elite Confederate army led by some of the most able military men in the country. This infusion of newly freed black slaves into the Union army, fighting for their freedom and hoping for equality, is what tipped the scales in the Union army's favor. Additionally, the Negro's thirst for knowledge, evidenced by a voracious appetite to become literate, was an indication that perhaps blacks were not the dim witted, sub-human beasts of burden portrayed by white Anglo-Saxons in Europe and the States.

> *... there was never an intent to give the Negro rights or equality commensurate with the white man.*

Finally, there was the tacit acknowledgment by executive and military leaders that the Negro was the driving force which made the modernization and industrialization of the United States possible. As historian Edward Baptist reveals in *The Half Has Never Been Told*, "In a single lifetime, the South grew from a narrow strip of worn out tobacco plantations to a continental cotton empire, and the United States grew into a modern, industrial, and capitalist economy."[12] Although there was an acknowledgment by most northerners that the atrocities of slavery were wrong, there was never an intent to give the Negro rights or equality commensurate with the white man.

After the issuance of Special Field Order 15 by General Sherman, which set aside 400,000 acres of land along the South Carolina, Georgia, and Florida coast for freed Negro slaves, it might appear that this country had momentarily found its moral compass. The perception that America was ready to move ahead with a new sense of purpose in its stated quest to provide fairness and opportunity for the Negro's integration into society was short lived, however. There were many whites who feared that providing equality to blacks would lead to their disenfranchisement and Negro supremacy. Consequently, after the assassination of Abraham Lincoln, President-elect Andrew Johnson began to seize on the rising anti-black sentiment and dismantle the legislation, executive orders, and other actions taken by the government to aid in the Negro's transition from slavery to freedom. With the stroke of a pen, President Johnson reversed Special Field Order 15, also known as "40 Acres and a Mule," along with the Freedman's Bureau and other government initiatives. Mr. Johnson's actions effectively returned lands confiscated and reallocated during the Civil War back to the southern plantation owners and Confederates who now sought to exact vengeance against the Negro—the easiest and most visible target for losing the Civil War. This was the catalyst for a period of lawlessness and anti-black sentiment, which produced the Ku Klux Klan (KKK), White Citizens Councils, and other organizations whose sole purpose was to intimidate, murder, and turn back the clock of progress for the Negro.

There is a similar anti-black revolt taking place now in this country being disguised with terms such as the "Tea Party," States Rights," and "Balancing the Budget."

This anti-black revolt was fueled in part by fear of a black rise in social, economic, and political power. During Reconstruction, there were more black senators and state representatives than any time in this country's history. Whites in the South and the North were fearful that black progress would threaten white prosperity and economic superiority. As a result, the period after Reconstruction saw a meteoric rise in Negro murders, Jim Crow, and white supremacist rhetoric and actions, which nullified and reversed many of the economic and political gains of the newly freed Negro. There is a similar anti-black revolt taking place now in this country, being disguised with terms such as the "Tea Party," "States Rights," and "Balancing the Budget."

The actions and inactions of federal and state legislatures since the election of Barack Obama as President are painfully reminiscent of actions taken during and after the death of Reconstruction. Evident are the legislative blocks to the Obama agenda, prophetically voiced by Rush Limbaugh and the political right. After the Presidential inauguration of 2008, Limbaugh unabashedly proclaimed, "I hope he fails." This sentiment, though not expressed in such direct terms by the Republican-led Senate, is clearly shown by their actions in stalling almost every major initiative put forth by the President since his inauguration. The blatant disrespect for the office of the President and the man holding it is unprecedented in the annals of U.S. history. We all know the reason but are too afraid to say it. The reason Mr. Obama has been treated with such disrespect is due to the color of his skin. Obama is black.

The escalation in police brutality and murder of unarmed black males also harkens back to the lawlessness of post-Reconstruction ...

From the framers of the Constitution to the architects of democracy, it was never envisioned or intended that a black man would hold the nation's highest office. Now that a black man is in the White House, it has caused a full-scale panic among the white Americans, giving rise to the extreme political right and movements like the Tea Party and other right-wing groups who have vowed to "take their country back." Mr. Obama's election has also mobilized and revitalized other fringe movements by white supremacist and "survivalist" organizations who view black progress as a threat to their domination. The escalation in police brutality and murder of unarmed black males also harkens back to the lawlessness of post-Reconstruction and seems eerily reminiscent of a time when blacks were either preyed upon or not protected by law enforcement.

The backlash against perceived or imagined black progress is nothing new. History reveals that whenever whites perceive black progress as a threat to the natural order of white supremacy, there is a social and political backlash. This is done by a myriad of tactics, which include playing to the fears of white America through the use of propaganda and exaggerated threats of black lawlessness, which necessitate forceful constraints by judicial and extra-judicial authorities. The war on drugs, the war on welfare fraud, the war on deadbeat dads, and the rise of documented police killings of young black men are all examples of how the politicians and wealthy power brokers control public opinion through misinformation and propaganda. All lies. This in turn, influences legislative and judicial action that has the effect of reversing black progress and eliminating the perceived threat of a rising black populace.

The State of the American Negro

Originally posted February 20, 2015

As I sit and ponder the state of the American Negro on the eve of President Obama's State of the Union address and the anniversary of the death of civil rights icon Martin Luther King, Jr., I am perplexed and amazed at how television personalities and others speak of the struggle for racial equality by the African American as something that has already been achieved. They talk of the civil rights movement and the quest for black liberation in the past tense, as if Dr. King's dream of equality has been realized. They use terms like blacks "were denied" and African Americans "have achieved" as though the majority of people in this country have overcome the scourge of racism and white supremacy. The factual reality of racial prejudice being alive and well in this country belies these propagandistic lies and half-truths, which serve as a smoke-screen to hide the ugly truth about the state of racial affairs in this country. Although many have bled, died, and suffered for the basic freedoms guaranteed by the Constitution of the United States, the truth of the matter is that, as Malcolm X once said, "in America, democracy is hypocrisy."

Although Jim Crow—a racial caste system where unequal treatment under the law was upheld for decades as acceptable and justified—has fallen due to the persistent struggle of the last three generations, discrimination and racial prejudice continues in its reinvented form. By legal necessity, racism has undergone a makeover. While blatant in-your-face discrimination against blacks under color of law and oppressive state legal statutes over-ruled by the supremacy of federal law has receded, the spirit—if not the letter—of Jim Crow still remains in the hearts and minds of many white Americans. The evidence of these truths is overwhelming, and one need look no further than the federal legislation over the last decade, which has served to extract and detract the safety nets and other social governmental programs designed to aid the African American in the quest for equality in education, employment, and housing. Government initiatives like Head Start, Aid for Families with Dependent Children, unemployment insurance, affirmative action, food stamps, and others have all been slashed to the point of ineffectiveness, if not altogether eliminated. Likewise, federal campaigns like the War on Drugs, the War on deadbeat dads, and the War on crime have all served to target and disproportionately impact black people, resulting in the loss of liberty and economic viability.

There is an organized effort by white acade\micians and lobbyists to abolish our HBCUs under the twisted rationale that they are no longer necessary or desired ...

Black institutions of higher education, once beacons of hope and many times the only hope of education for millions of African Americans, now are closing at a rapid rate and struggling to keep the doors open due to decreased endowments and support from state governments. Historically Black Colleges and Universities (HBCUs) are suffering and dying while white colleges continue to grow and thrive with their multimillion and billion-dollar endowments from wealthy white benefactors and state and local governments. These same state and local governments, which used to provide a pittance of support to black colleges before desegregation, now turn a blind eye to their financial need. At the same time, there is an organized effort by white academicians and lobbyists to abolish our HBCUs under the twisted rationale that they are no longer necessary or desired due to the advent of desegregation and the decrease in student enrollment on Black college campuses. A larger lie has never been told.

The truth is that white colleges were never constructed or intended to serve the peculiar and particular needs of the intellectually and culturally deprived and despised American Negro. This is a role that only the HBCU embraced and fulfilled with overwhelming success for nearly a century before the walls of separate but equal were abolished by *Brown v. Board of Education of Topeka* in 1954 and the federal intervention of the National Guard on the campuses of Little Rock's Central High School in 1957 and the University of Alabama in 1963.

Even today, in 2015, as the enrollment of more black students at white universities continues to rise, the black student is only tolerated in a white college culture that neither nurtures nor embraces them. Black athletes are inspected and prized like specimens of cattle or slaves on the auction block, being readied for the modern day equivalent of gladiators, for the purpose and privilege of financial exploitation, all to the glory of white universities. Meanwhile, the non-athletes are merely tolerated in an Anglo-European culture that speaks not to the traditions and customs of the African American. They are forced to carve out and establish a niche within a culture that is mostly inhospitable. Just like in the larger American society, blacks are a subculture within a culture, trapped in the "double consciousness" of being not fully American and not fully African. We are caught somewhere in the middle of a bifurcated existence—displaced from our homeland and African heritage but unable to fully cross the bridge of acceptance in America while separated by the ocean of white supremacy.

In the words of Carter G. Woodson, "That's miseducation."

Integration has failed, and the evidence is borne out by the fact that most inner-city public schools are still segregated. Furthermore, its failure is documented by the increasing rates of Black high school drop- outs, where in some areas of the nation are as high as five out of eight for black males. Most inner-city schools are filled with black kids and black teachers but controlled by the bureaucracy of white school boards and administrators. These white administrators and government officials intentionally live in the suburbs and send their children to predominantly white schools while building new and pristine edifices outside the city limits in newly incorporated townships outside the reach of urban blight and blackness. This takes place while the inner-city public education of the Negro serves only to perpetuate our dependence on—and further enrich—the institutions that deny us equal citizenship. That's not education. In the words of Carter G. Woodson, "that's miseducation."

The American Negro has defied all odds and survived the Middle Passage, over 300 years of slavery, Jim Crow, and systemic and structural racism. The notion that the African American is dependent on the federal government due to laziness and a trifle nature does not square with history or the facts. This was disproven during slavery, the antebellum and post antebellum south, and through pre- and post-Reconstruction. Our equitable demands on the federal government are due to the inequality of opportunity in all phases of American society. The gap is too wide and the economic disparities too entrenched and systemic to remedy with government programs and self-help alone. The chasm of white supremacy and racism is too deep. Black people are owed reparations for the centuries of slave labor that changed America's economic trajectory.

Give us what is owed ... this is the only solution to the centuries-old problem of the inequality of the races.

Slavery is the economic bedrock of this country. America was built and prospered on the free labor of our African ancestors. For this, the descendants of slaves should be paid for the trillions of dollars in economic prosperity which has benefitted the Anglo-European families and institutions but has escaped the American Negro. Give blacks what is justifiably owed for the centuries of free slave labor and for the millions of wrongful deaths that occurred during and after the transatlantic slave trade. African Americans are owed the dignity and independence that comes from economic empowerment. Give us what is owed, and we can buy our own land, build our own institutions, and deal with Anglo-Europeans on equal financial footing. This is the only solution to the centuries-old problem of the inequality of the races.

Over 150 years after The Emancipation Proclamation … over 60 years after *Brown v. Board of Education of Topeka* … 38 years after the assassination of Dr. Martin Luther King, Jr. … six years after the election of President Barack Obama … has the Negro made it? Has the Negro achieved racial, social, and economic equality in this so-called land of the free?

The answer is an unequivocal and resounding NO!

Will King's dream of a colorblind society ever be realized in America, where men are judged by the content of their character and not the color of their skin? The answer is an equally unequivocal and resounding NO!

Now that we've settled those questions now and forever let's begin the serious talk of a remedy for the centuries of free slave labor, murder, and dehumanization suffered by the Negro, which spawned the greatest economic turnaround in world history. The answer is Reparations, and the time is now!

K. Gerald Torrence

Obama's Refusal to Get It Right on Racism

Originally posted April 21, 2015

As the evidence continues to mount across America showing a pervasive and increasingly blatant manifestation of racism in all of its varied and virulent forms, the nation's first black President's acknowledgment and response has been, at best, cautious and, at worst, non-existent. This is a curious anomaly since President Obama himself has been the target of racist jokes and disrespect, treated like a nigger from the first day he took office. Recent racist emails directed at the President and the First Lady, Michelle Obama, underscore this point.

President Obama's continued silence regarding the seeming domino effect of the killing of unarmed black men by white police officers could not be more deafening. Aren't Presidents, no matter the color, duty-bound to condemn publicly and vociferously acts that appear to be an undeclared open season on the lives of Black men? My question is whether the current President's reticence to speak out on racial issues is purely political or much deeper than that.

Understandably, the President is between a rock and a hard place regarding race because, as a black man, he must represent the interests of all Americans, the majority of which are of European descent. This quandary notwithstanding, it does the quest for justice in America for African Americans a supreme disservice to overlook the obvious and downplay the factor of race and racism at play in every segment of American society. How long will President Obama publicly look the other way and ignore the obvious? In the history of this country, there has never been a President so vilified, insulted, and undermined by congressmen through action and inaction, which belie their claims of legitimate policy differences. Policy issues aside, President Obama has never been given the respect and the dignity that the office of the President deserves and which traditionally has been given to white office holders. Despite Mr. Obama's best efforts to be Presidential and avoid the scandal and improprieties of past presidents like Bill Clinton and a long list of others, he continues to bang his head against the stone wall of racial bigotry and white supremacy in America.

> *Perhaps this missing genealogical and cultural nexus is what prevents him from fully empathizing with the centuries-old struggle of the American Negro for racial equality.*

Dare I say that Mr. Obama's reluctance to embrace the worsening plight of African Americans in this country and to adopt our struggles as his own is due to his mixed heritage and ancestry. Could it be that by having an African father (Barack Hussein Obama, Sr.), who was born in Kenya's Nyanza province, and a mother of Irish and German ancestry, he is disconnected and desensitized to the culture and historical suffering of the American Negro? Although educated in America, Obama Sr. was of distinctly African heritage, belonging to an ethnic group called the Luo which makes up Kenya's third largest ethnic group. Neither of Mr. Obama's parents share a lineage—historical, cultural, or otherwise—connected to African Americans whose ancestors came over on slave ships. Likewise, Mr. Obama's ancestors never suffered the psychological trauma, brutality, and degradation of slavery, Jim Crow, and the civil rights struggles of the 1960s. As a black man here in America, Mr. Obama is certainly a beneficiary of those struggles, but he has no lineal connection. Perhaps this missing genealogical and cultural nexus is what prevents him from fully empathizing with the centuries-old struggle of the American Negro for racial equality.

Furthermore, I would argue that skin color alone does not determine racial identity. There are countless examples throughout history where fair-skinned black people tried to pass as white and where dark-skinned Negroes sought to shake off the shackles of skin color by seeking to assimilate into white culture as if color didn't matter. As Obama and others before him have undoubtedly learned, race in the United States of America has always mattered. It is still the yardstick for the subjective measure of human worth in this country, acknowledged by the controlling majority or not.

Well, Mr. Obama, if you won't say it, I will say it for you. The United States of America is the most racist country in the world, notwithstanding your election as President. In fact, your election has only served to exacerbate and bring to the surface the latent racial animus that white folk still hold for black people in this country. We can never effectively devise a solution as long as we fail and refuse to recognize the problem. The ostrich approach of burying our heads in the sand will not make the problem of racism go away. Yes, America. We have a problem. Racism is alive, well, and arguably on the rise in this country, and unless we are honest about its existence, we remain powerless to effectively address it.

Mr. President, we must honestly face the problems of racism and the culture of white supremacy which still plague this country. Your refusal to acknowledge or address the systemic and pervasive nature of racism in America only serves to perpetuate the problem. By doing and saying nothing, you give tacit approval to the status quo, thereby enabling the continued oppression of African Americans.

The Movement Behind the Massacre

Originally posted July 15, 2015

Days after the church massacre that killed nine African American worshipers at the historic Emmanuel A.M.E. Church in Charleston, South Carolina, President Obama finally acknowledged the existence of racism. He is to be commended. It was important that this public acknowledgment come from our nation's first (and last) black President. The question remains, however, as to what took him so long. It's unfortunate that it took the murder of nine innocent and blameless black churchgoers by 21-year-old avowed white supremacist Dylann Roof to prompt Mr. Obama's belated acknowledgment. The fact that one of the murdered victims was South Carolina State Senator Clementa Pinckney no doubt raised the profile of this horrific slaughter, making the implications far more difficult to ignore.

If there were ever an emphatic exclamation point to the proliferation of far-right white supremacist organizations and their sympathizers who advocate death and destruction to African Americans, this was it. Ironically, it appears that Roof's diabolical and sinister actions come in response and as a retort to the Black Lives Matter campaign, which protested the rash of killings of unarmed black men at the hands of white police officers. The brazen and cowardly massacre at the historic Emmanuel A.M.E. Church was a thunderbolt which gave the truest indication of the smoldering undercurrent of anti- African American sentiment present in this country.

The words "hate crime" don't begin to adequately describe the heinous act of terrorism committed at "Mother Emmanuel," so called because of its historical significance as the first independent black denomination in the nation. Founded in 1816 by the Reverend Morris Brown and Denmark Vesey (the architect of "The Rising," a major slave revolt in Charleston in 1822), Emmanuel's significance in the African American struggle for equality is undeniable. Although Vesey was quickly judged guilty and hanged along with five other slaves deemed central to the planned revolt, the courage, and fortitude demonstrated in their fight for freedom is forever tied to Emmanuel. It is indeed ironic that almost 200 years later, Emmanuel again takes center stage in the African American struggle for freedom and equality.

This most recent church massacre is eerily reminiscent of the black church bombing that took place at the 16th Street Baptist Church in Birmingham, Alabama, on Sunday, September 15, 1963. Dr. Martin Luther King, Jr. described the act as "one of the most vicious and tragic crimes ever perpetrated against humanity," as the explosion at the church killed four girls and injured 22 others. Although an FBI investigation in 1965 concluded the church bombing had been committed by four known Ku Klux Klansmen and segregationists, no prosecutions ensued until more than 22 years later.

Just as the 16th Street Baptist Church bombing marked a turning point in the African American Civil Rights Movement in the 1960s, this most recent terrorist act by white supremacist Dylann Roof must signal a turning point. A point in which American society turns and pivots away from the false and self-serving propaganda, suggesting a color blind society where race no longer matters. A bigger lie has never been told, yet the forces of the empire and its operatives continue to deceive the populace as to the continuing governmental and societal oppression of African Americans.

Roof's chilling words, "I came to shoot black people," gives unambiguous validation to the New America Foundation's (NAF) recent findings that "White Americans are a bigger terror threat than Islamic extremists." (NAF is a nonprofit, nonpartisan public policy institute and think tank.) A new study by the Foundation confirms that white Americans have killed more people in attacks than Muslims or any other group in the last fourteen years. The Foundation's research found that of the 26 attacks on U.S. soil defined as acts of terror since September 11, 2001, 19 of those were committed by non-Muslims. This study further concluded that radical Islamists were indicted more frequently than non-Muslim extremists and served longer sentences. Likewise, the hunt for foreign terrorists in Afghanistan and other countries in the Middle East is given the highest military and law enforcement priority, while homegrown white supremacists and extremists get essentially a governmental "pass" to indoctrinate, infiltrate, and perpetuate acts of extreme violence and hatred against blacks living here in this country.

Furthermore, the proliferation of white hate groups is not just a national movement; it's an international one that coincides with the anti- immigration push by Western nations such as Great Britain, France, and Germany. The influx of Africans, Middle Easterners, and other dark skinned peoples fleeing conflict in their native land onto European shores has helped galvanize the message of white genocide, feeding the growth of white nationalism worldwide. It is dangerously naive to conclude that Roof is some deranged psychopath, alone in his perverted view that blacks are somehow taking over the country and need to be stopped by the threat of violence and murder. Quite to the contrary, 21- year-old Dylann Roofs' thought processes and dangerous ideology were learned and cultivated through a network of white supremacist websites which promote the re-establishment of complete white control of the United States.

While these seemingly dormant voices of white supremacy are not new, they have continued to gain traction since the election of Barak Obama as President.

Here again, history is only repeating itself. This same message was widely circulated and well received by both Northerners and Southerners during the Reconstruction period after the Civil War. In fact, the view was so widely held that it precipitated the premature end of Reconstruction and the ushering in of the Jim Crow era. While these seemingly dormant voices of white supremacy are not new, they have continued to gain traction since the election of Barack Obama as President.

Now is the time for a new interpretation of existing federal legislation which will classify right-wing white supremacist groups such as the Ku Klux Klan, the Skinheads, the Aryan Nation, the Council of Conservative Citizens, and others as terrorist organizations subject to arrest and prosecution for advocating violence or encouraging others to join their ranks. The time is now because these homegrown terrorist and other subversive groups are a bigger threat to the peace and security of America than ISIS ever could be half a world away. I'm calling on the President and Congress to expand the USA PATRIOT Act—Uniting and Strengthening America by Providing Appropriate Tools Required to Intercept and Obstruct Terrorism Act of 2001—to include white supremacist groups that continue to plot and plan for the death and destruction of African Americans. The PATRIOT Sunsets Extensions Act of 2011, a four-year extension of three key provisions in the USA PATRIOT Act which provides for roving wiretaps, searches of business records, and conducting surveillance of "lone wolves" (i.e., individuals suspected of terrorist-related activities not linked to terrorist groups), should equally apply to white supremacist groups who advocate for the subversion of the rule of law in the name of white primacy.

If the President and Congress are really serious about the war on terror, then the battle against it must be waged right here at home.

If the U.S. government is truly serious about its "War on Terror," the fight must also be waged here at home against white supremacists and their organizations, which sow seeds of hate, violence, and governmental overthrow. Enough with the double standard. A terrorist is a terrorist, whether they wear a thobe (long robe worn by some Muslims) or the white robe of the KKK. The resulting death and horror is the same, so the risk and the threat to African Americans should be taken just as seriously by federal authorities. We must demand that the President and Congress act immediately to end the hypocrisy and double standard regarding terrorism, whether it's committed by Islamic Jihadists or white supremacists. If the President and Congress are really serious about the war on terror, then the battle against it must be waged right here at home.

K. Gerald Torrence

Since when are Egyptians not white? All I know are.

Rupert Murdoch

RACISM AND THE MEDIA

Death of Another Black Icon

Originally posted November 25, 2014

The recent avalanche of tawdry allegations directed at African American icon Bill Cosby resurrects feelings of profound loss akin to the deaths of Maya Angelou, Martin Luther King, Jr., and Malcolm X. Although Cosby's demise is not a physical death, it certainly feels like the larger-than-life persona we knew and loved for almost half a century is gone forever. The scurrilous attacks on Cosby, however, follow a dangerous and alarming trend. In recent weeks and months, we have witnessed an almost continuous parade of black men being plastered across the television screens as networks saturate the airwaves with stories of alleged violence and lawlessness against women and kids.

The recent attacks on Cosby's heretofore sterling reputation by fifty-seven white and black women, who now claim rape and sexual misconduct in some cases thirty years later, doesn't pass the smell test. In fact, it stinks to high heaven of racism and cultural genocide. If white America, through its cadre of cable news networks and endless supply of opinionated sycophants, can sully and smear the legacy of a man of Cosby's accomplishments without so much of a word of protest, then we as black folks have lost not just the battle but also the war. With one fell swoop, an endearing and enduring legacy of black pride and accomplishment has been destroyed. With Cosby's destruction comes one more nail in the coffin of the African American male's battered and tattered perception of respectability.

Whether Cosby is guilty as charged is anybody's guess. Far be it from me to decide Cosby's guilt or innocence. What we do know is that throughout America's history, black men have been falsely accused of sexual misconduct involving white women and paid with their lives at the hands of mob and vigilante injustice. Untold numbers of African American men have been lynched and murdered for "wayward eyes" and the mere suspicion of consorting with white women. I guess Mr. Cosby should be thankful it's 2014 and not 1914. If so, this discussion and the aftermath would undoubtedly be much different.

There are those who legitimately raise the question of the likelihood of all fifty-seven women lying. I don't know, but stranger things have happened. It's certainly not beyond the realm of possibility. This is especially true considering the questionable timing of the allegations—in some cases, thirty years later. Among the most vociferous of Cosby's accusers is Janice Dickinson, whose years of admitted and well-chronicled drug-fueled lifestyle is the stuff of legend. Dickinson's past and questionable choices in voluntarily taking a pill allegedly offered by Cosby raise serious questions about her credibility. Whatever the case, I believe that Mr. Cosby has earned over a lifetime of achievement and public service and at least the right of discretionary pause by those in the mainstream media who would so quickly rush to judgment.

Cable News' Attempts to Shape Public Opinion

Originally posted December 22, 2014

As the avalanche of evidence continues to accrue, exposing the deepening racial divide in this country, the mythological concept of a post-racial society must be exposed as the propagandistic farce that it is.

The nonexistential notion that America has miraculously moved past considerations of human worth and value is a fallacy propagated by those who would seek to maintain the status quo. These gatekeepers of white supremacy and spin doctors who would echo these untruths are the direct enemy of black liberation and progress. To believe that the handpicked Negroes that the mainstream media presents to us as authoritative symbols of black consciousness would intentionally dupe us into believing that Dr. King's dream of freedom for the Negro has been achieved might be, for some, a tough pill to swallow. Let's examine the evidence.

They point to the Civil Rights Act of 1964, the Voting Rights Act, the so-called integration of public schools, and the election of a black President as proof positive that racial equality has been achieved. Yes, these scripted talking heads with a vested interest in misleading the masses would have us believe that since we now have a few high-profile black millionaires in areas of entertainment and professional sports, we now have a level playing field where all are judged without regard to skin color. This is nonsense!

Who are these fabricators and manipulators of reality, and what America are they living in? Well, whenever white folk want to confuse and distract through subterfuge and deception, they use a black face to deliver the message. I say kill the messengers! (Not literally.) The black CNN anchors of the world do more to set back the cause of black truth than thousands of racist KKK flyers about the dangers of race mixing and predatory black men. Instead, the wealthy white disseminators of news use carefully selected and crafted models of Negro intellectualism to promote the messages of peace and moderation. While appearing to air the views of a diverse audience through the use of black faces, the public is actually being led down a primrose path that has been carefully created and orchestrated by the gatekeepers of public opinion.

These modern-day Negroes are the latest reincarnation of sellouts and Uncle Toms, who wittingly and unwittingly use their platforms of visibility and perceived credibility to do the master's bidding. Those who masquerade as journalists while pushing theirs and the oppressor's agenda are a grave threat to the cause of black liberation. We must recognize this trickery and deception for what it is. These so- called black social and political analysts, who sometimes wear three and four hats of anchor, reporter, analyst, and social commentator, must be exposed for who they are. They do not speak for black people and are incapable of doing so! No one "can serve two masters."

This parade of black talking heads on cable news networks who ostensibly speak for the African American while sitting at the master's table well fed and satisfied are exploited and compromised beyond usefulness. They know not the frustrations and realities of the black man or woman on the street who must eat, sleep, and breathe the daily indignation of 21st century racism. No, they don't represent me or the vast majority of African Americans they purport to speak for.

How long will we allow the oppressor to choose our leaders and handpick our spokespersons based on their own self-serving interests while compromising their integrity with high profile visibility and fat pay checks? (Yes, I am talking about you, Al Sharpton, and Don

Lemon.) When will we recognize these vultures for who they are, picking the bones of each and every new crisis in the black community, real or imagined, while in many cases placing their own financial and professional interests above the integrity of the positions they take and the stories they cover.

K. Gerald Torrence

Supreme Ignorance Is Not Confined to the Poor and Uneducated

Originally posted January 31, 2015

Rupert Murdoch, the executive chairman of the News Corporation, which owns 21st Century Fox, Fox News, and the *Wall Street Journal*, recently displayed his supreme ignorance when responding to criticism surrounding the studio's decision to cast all of the main characters in the movie *Exodus: Gods and Kings* as white. Murdoch, one of the richest and most influential men in the world, recently wrote on Twitter: "Since when are Egyptians not white? All I know are."

Wow. If it weren't for Murdoch's enormous wealth, power, and influence, his words might be comical. Considering, however, that Murdoch is the founder, Chairman, and CEO of the global media holding company News Corporation, the world's second-largest media conglomerate influencing and shaping the information that millions of Americans are fed every day, his comments are indeed scary. According to Forbes' 2013 list of richest Americans, Murdoch is the 33rd richest person in the U.S. and the 91st richest in the world, with a net worth of $13.4 billion. In 2014, Forbes ranked "Rupert Murdoch & Family" as the 33rd most powerful person in the world. How is it that a man educated in one of the most respected European institutions in the world—Worcester College dating back to 1283 as Gloucester College—can be so ignorant and out of touch with established and accepted principles of history and geography? Perhaps the answer lies in the question. Europeans, for centuries have written and rewritten world history in order to edify themselves and their culture at the expense of truth and factual accountability.

Of course, European revisionist history is nothing new. The conqueror has always written his account of world events to reflect his truth while subjugating the vanquished peoples' customs and cultural contributions to society. This type of propaganda and misinformation goes all the way back to Alexander the Great, King James, and the first translation of the *Holy Bible*. Important language and voices were muted, omitted, and selectively given significance based on the political, social, and military objectives of the oppressor. Consequently, much of recorded history was written from the jaded and biased perspectives of the Greeks and Romans for the purpose of self- glorification without regard to facts or historical accuracy.

Well, Mr. Murdoch, despite your Worcester College, University of Oxford education, it is my sad duty to inform you that Egypt is in Africa! Your words and your ignorance are the most poignant and profound indictment of European-based thought and learning in recent memory. This type of ignorance is primarily responsible for the perpetuation of centuries of untruths and misinformation about Africa, its people, and its legacy. These false teachings continue to rob Africa and its descendants of the truth about their rich history and heritage. What a travesty indeed that lies such as these still reverberate in the 21st century and serve to keep the myth of white supremacy alive and well!

The early Christians were Africans with black skin—not Europeans with blonde hair and blue eyes.

The cinematic portrayals of Moses, Jesus, and other characters of the *Holy Bible* as white does not square with geographical or historical accuracy. The historical Jesus was not European. The Bible says he "had hair like lamb's wool and feet like burnished brass." Neither of these features fit the modern day Anglo-European depiction of Jesus or his followers. Egypt, the so-called "Middle East," and modern day Israel are geographically located in North Africa. It's time we started teaching the truth about the history of Africa as the cradle of civilization and the birthplace of Christianity and organized religion. The early Christians were Africans with black skin—not Europeans with blonde hair and blue eyes.

The decision by Egyptian authorities to ban the showing of the Exodus film because it "asserts historical falsehoods and a Zionist view" is welcome and long overdue. Of course, it will take decades to reverse the centuries of European misrepresentation and false characterization of historical truths regarding Africa and biblical history, but it's past time that we began the process.

No, Mr. Murdoch, Europeans did not build the pyramids.

Africans did.

Baltimore and Beyond …
The Crisis Beneath the Crisis

Originally posted May 4, 2015

The wallpaper coverage of the recent eruption of unrest in Baltimore, which spawned a state of emergency and the presence of over 5,000 National Guardsmen and other law enforcement personnel, is an outward manifestation of a crisis of oppression that has gone unchecked for decades—if not centuries—in this country. The devaluing of black lives by law enforcement and state and local governments, which began with the establishment of a Constitution that did not recognize the Negro as anything other than property, is the blueprint that still undergirds American jurisprudence. This separate and unequal treatment of black folk by governmental authorities, beginning with the police, the courts, and city governments, which oversee them, are conditions that have endured through and in spite of emancipation, civil rights struggles, and the passing of Federal laws designed to address them. The slow march of the Negro toward equal justice under the law has always been marked by police brutality, murder, and the ever-present cover-up by policy departments and government agencies to hide and insulate them from accountability for the atrocities precipitated against African Americans.

It is only now that we've entered the age of the digital camera phone and the "eyes in the sky" of video surveillance in every American city that the injustices against black and brown citizens are being unmasked. With the very public executions of Michael Brown, Eric

Garner, Freddie Gray, and a host of other black and unarmed men, the systemic targeting of African Americans by police and city governments has ignited the powder keg of simmering rage fueled by legal and economic oppression. Baltimore, like cities still yet to blow up, was simply a time bomb waiting to explode. The violent and lawless display in Baltimore by protesters is only a symptom of the ills of inequality and oppression of black folk by a system of unequal justice and treatment under the law, dating back to the era of Jim Crow, which defined and established a different set of applied rules and treatment depending on race. Although Jim Crow laws have been struck down, the spirit of these laws is still very much present in a system which is still operated and perpetuated by the great-grandsons and - granddaughters of former slave masters. Old traditions and established perceptions of black inferiority and white supremacy die very hard, if ever.

These young people are only a by-product ... a disposable drain on the financial coffers and patience of white America.

A pot that simmers—and simmers over a hot flame—will eventually boil over. These young black men and women are simply rising up against a system that offers them little justice and less opportunity. President Obama, Baltimore Mayor Stephanie Rawlings- Blake, and Maryland Governor Larry Hogan's references to the protesters as criminals and thugs is a poignant illustration of how the empire and those charged with its maintenance and operation perpetuate negative views of African American youth. How unfortunate indeed when black elected officials join the chorus of establishment voices in the devaluation and dehumanization of some of our misguided young brothers and sisters. The reckless use of terms like "thugs and criminals" has almost become a synonym with the "n" word, used throughout history to refer to the Negro's wretchedness. I suggest, however, that these terms are more applicable to the murderous white police officers responsible for the recent deaths of so many unarmed black men. This criminal and thug stereotype systemically applied to Black men is precisely what has been used to fuel the industrial prison complex and the economic benefit that inures to private investors and state and local governments. These young people are only a by-product of a system of federal, state, and local governments that views African Americans as a disposable drain on the financial coffers and patience of white America.

The empire and its news media conglomerates would have us focus our attention on the "rioting" and the destruction of property rather than the senseless killing of Freddie Gray and others. Take the example of Toya Graham, the black mother whose viral video looped endlessly on CNN as she relentlessly and repeatedly struck her 16-year-old son with an avalanche of blows to his face and head. Although the reaction to this violent spectacle by the single mother of six was met with applause and words of praise—from white and black news commentators alike—I can only imagine the feigned outrage and public outcry that would have ensued under any other circumstance. Oddly enough, there was not a peep of protest from the cable news pundits, the bleeding-heart liberals, or by any of those who are responsible for taking corporal punishment out of the home and the schools in black communities. Under any circumstance other than for the protection of the empire, its property, and its hypocritical values, such a beat down would have produced vehement outrage from white America, prompting immediate involvement by the state department of social services and criminal prosecution of Graham for domestic violence and child abuse.

These hypocrites, who condemned Adrian Peterson in principle for disciplining his child in the privacy of his home, are the same politically correct pundits and spin doctors whose position changes depending on the always questionable objectives of the empire and its news-media minions. Where are these bleeding-heart liberals who only months ago saturated the airwaves about domestic violence and child abuse, making the Black man the face of child abuse and domestic violence in the Peterson case and others? I believe it no coincidence that the nationwide assault on Black families by state departments of social services for physical discipline of our children is partly responsible for the epidemic rise of incarceration of young black men. Just another example of the empire taking away the authority of black parents to reign in wayward youth and provide discipline of our children at an early age. Here again, we have the ever-present double standard by white America. Corporal punishment/child abuse is okay when it involves protecting the empire, but criminal when it involves an attempt by black men to discipline their sons in the home.

I shudder to imagine the carnage that will result if the powder keg of oppression continues unabated, and finally erupts like a domino effect in cities across America.

Although I understand the frustration of the youth, their tactics of destruction and looting of the very neighborhoods and businesses that serve their communities is misguided at best. Furthermore, this lawless behavior plays right into the stereotype and the heavy hand of an already discriminatory criminal justice system. The more than 300 young people arrested and the hundreds more that face impending and possible arrest will be dealt with harshly by a corrupt judicial system that always protects the rights of the white landholder and relegates too many African Americans to a hopelessness and lack of opportunity feeding the American industrial prison complex. I shudder to imagine the carnage that will result if the powder keg of oppression continues unabated and finally erupts like a domino effect in cities across America.

We must now resist the temptation to put a band-aid on a systemic problem of lack of opportunity and hopelessness, which breeds contempt and lawlessness by a forgotten generation of young black kids. A total re-evaluation and reconstruction of the policies and priorities of government, which takes the boot of oppression from the necks of African Americans, is the only real solution. Otherwise, the Fergusons and Baltimores will only be the tip of the iceberg of confrontation of a culture that still treats African Americans—in words immortalized in the U.S. Constitution and by former Chief Justice Roger B. Taney—as "three fifths of a person … with no rights which the white man is bound to respect."

K. Gerald Torrence

The very statement that black lives matter underscores the absurdity of the question implicit in the statement. By even having to say it, we call into question the value and relative worth of African American life here in the United States ... The devaluation of black lives is rooted and steeped in history ...

K. Gerald Torrence
August 2015
"The (Not So) Curious Case of Sandra Bland"

BLACK LIVES MATTER

The Color of Justice

Originally posted December 6, 2014

The continuing aftermath and ongoing discussions about what constitutes justice in the tragic police shootings of unarmed black teenager Michael Brown and the choking death of Eric Garner begs the question: what is justice, and what is its color? The notion of a color blind justice system is not a novel one. Whether African Americans could realistically hope for true equality in this country is a debate that goes back to the earliest black scholars and educators, such as W.E.B. DuBois and Booker T. Washington. Sadly, this debate still rages over one hundred fifty years after the Emancipation Proclamation and more than fifty years after *Brown v. Board of Education* ostensibly ended racial discrimination in this country.

To the vast majority of whites, justice was served by the grand jury's decision not to indict the white police officers responsible for the deaths of Mike Brown and Eric Garner. To most African Americans, the police shooting of the unarmed black males smells with the familiar rotten stench of decades-old police oppression and predatory behavior in the black community. This systematic and endemic brutality by white law enforcement officers against unarmed and defenseless African Americans far too often ends in black males being murdered for questionable offenses. What's most telling is the divergence of opinion on whether justice was achieved, depending on the race of whom you ask … white or black. The majority of whites feel that justice was served with the grand jury non-indictments, while blacks overwhelmingly feel that these decisions represent more of the same historic devaluing of black lives in America.

Of course, this devaluation of black life is nothing new in this country. In fact, it dates all the way back to the founding fathers' draft of the U.S. Constitution in 1787. In the definitive document of American government and citizens' rights, the Negro is only described as chattel or property, devoid of citizenship, representing only 3/5 of a man for purposes of quantification and valuation. With this ignominious definition of the Negro worth, is it any wonder that even today, centuries later, the value of Negro life is less than that of whites? This should be a surprise to no one.

Donald Sterling gave the world a peek into the secret thoughts of the rich and powerful white men who run this country …

You can't legislate away centuries of structural racism and systemic white supremacy with the stroke of a pen or the passing of laws. The bedrock-ingrained attitudes of white superiority run too deep and are passed down from generation to generation, despite what the politically correct pundits and politicians might mouth when the cameras are rolling. But what do they say amongst themselves under the cloak of presumed secrecy? Donald Sterling gave the world a peek into the secret thoughts of the rich and powerful white men who run this country, although his racist remarks were dismissed as an anomaly by those media conglomerates who would seek to perpetuate the charade of a color blind, post-racial society.

The truth is, racism in this country is alive and as potent as ever, despite and in spite of the election of a so-called "Black President." The color of justice, just like the color of everything else in America, was always intended to be white. From the framers of the Constitution to the Presidents, Congress, judges, prosecutors, juries, police officers, universities, and institutions of finance and commerce, these stewards of justice and liberty have always been white. The integration of a darkie here or there for token appearances can't and hasn't changed the fact that America is a country built and constructed for the benefit of the white race, who, at heart, want to perpetuate the privilege passed down from their European ancestors—those ancestors who, through larceny and murder, decimated the Native American population to near extinction. There is no problem as long as those from whom the land was stolen and those upon whose backs the economy was built don't try to upset what they consider the natural order of things. The equation is and always will be white over non-white.

The recent unrest in Ferguson, Missouri, and New York is only a symptom of the much larger problem of inequality of the races and the perpetuation of white supremacy. At the end of the day, any supremacy is always maintained by force. The violence and brutality against blacks in this country dates back to its founding. The latest evidence of white and black polarization is only an indication of the simmering racial tensions that lie just beneath the surface, which have only been exacerbated by the election of President Barack Obama. There is still much resentment and disdain toward blacks in this country by a majority of whites who feel that they are losing control. The failure and unwillingness of white and so-called black leaders to face this reality is part and parcel of the problem. We continue to kick this can down the road and pretend that racism doesn't exist or that it is not a problem. Yes, racism exists, and it's bad … very bad. It seems the more things have changed, the more they remain the same. Consequently, the question of justice in America, as well as its color, is still a matter of black and white.

K. Gerald Torrence

Uncle Toms in Blue

Originally posted May 8, 2015

Even more disturbing than the rash of publicly-exposed killings of unarmed black men by white cops is the oftentimes presence of black cops who are witnesses and accessories to the murder and the cover-up. These black police officers who turn a blind eye and abet the racist white cops who kill and victimize members of their own race are despicable cowards who should be exposed and prosecuted along with their racist white counterparts.

In my view, there are always two crimes: first comes the murder or the brutality, and then comes the cover-up. Black police officers who sit idly by and say nothing or do nothing are just as guilty as if they had pulled the trigger themselves. In fact, their complicity may be worse in perpetuating the genocide of their own people. What other race of people does that, other than the Americanized Negro? Instead of standing up for what's right, they stand up for what's white, despite the harsh consequences to their own people. These post-antebellum subservient officers of the empire are the modern-day incarnation of the stereotypical Uncle Tom characters from slavery who will do anything to please the master, even if it means participating in a system of oppression and brutality that perpetuates the subjugation of their race. Like the biblical character Judas, all of this is done for a few pieces of silver. Are a badge and a uniform a fair exchange for the lives of our young people and the already bleak future of millions of African Americans?

Just as in any profession, there is a mixture of both good and bad. However, no one can say with any degree of certainty whether there is a preponderance of good police officers or what the actual ratio of good to bad is. This is the great unknown. My guess is somewhere around 50-50. There is no way to know for sure, but I'm sick and tired of the politically correct pundits and the social media's characterization of "a few bad officers." Almost every black man in this country has had at least one unfortunate encounter with a racist white cop or an overzealous black one. Many times, the black officers are worse than the white in their often heavy-handed approach to the performance of their duties when dealing with members of our community. This reality belies the always conservative estimates of the news media and those who have never been victimized by rogue police officers.

If these so-called "good" police officers are not a part of the solution, then they are part of the problem.

Having said that, how do we categorize those police officers, white or black, who may not be guilty by commission but are guilty by omission through their indifference and apathy to crimes being committed by other officers of whom they have direct or indirect knowledge? After all, law enforcement is a job that should epitomize the highest standards of honor and morality. I suggest that cops who assist in the cover-up of police misconduct and who help maintain the "blue wall of silence" with respect to police criminality are guilty themselves as aiders or abettors, if not outright conspirators. I can't consider those who condone police misconduct by looking the other way as "good police officers." If these so-called "good" police officers are not a part of the solution, then they are part of the problem.

The only solution to the centuries-old endemic and systemic culture of police brutality and the devaluation of black life by those who are sworn to serve and protect is to tear it down then rebuild and restructure from the bottom up. This will undoubtedly necessitate a complete purge of police departments across this nation, getting rid of those who hide their criminality and indifference behind a badge and a gun, shielded from accountability by a system that for too long has served as a perpetrator of injustice instead of a force to promote justice.

Unfortunately, the old plantation slave mentality is still very much alive and thriving among African Americans over 150 years after Emancipation. This is a testament to the effectiveness and the complete psychological, social, and cultural divestment of the enslaved Africans from their natural inclination to love themselves and their people. The Negro slave, instead, was systematically broken down and disconnected from all things familiar and, by necessity, forced to look to the white man for all things necessary for survival. Consequently, survival often meant participation and complicity in the slave master's mission of brutality, death, and denigration of other Negro slaves.

We have been conditioned to see ourselves as the white man sees us: inferior and unworthy of respect and dignity as a people ...

The willingness of some modern-day African Americans to be compliant in the genocide of our own people by the same oppressive system that denies us all equality offers a strange dichotomy. By subjugating our own people in the name of the empire, we destroy the future of our race by perpetuating a system that keeps us in bondage. We then become "good Negroes." Faithful and loyal servants to the empire, who by our toil and our sweat, promote the continuation of institutions which serve as the foundation of our inequality. We, black people, are still so psychologically dependent on the white man for survival—to give us a job or give us a position of perceived status—that we willingly compromise all principles of basic morality when it comes to the mistreatment of people who look like us. We have been conditioned to see ourselves as the white man sees us: inferior and unworthy of respect and dignity as a people. Consequently, it is easier for us to go along to get along with white folks and adopt their twisted notions of right and wrong, even when it amounts to self-hate and self- destruction, resulting in the death, denigration, and continuing oppression of the African American.

The solution, then, is two-fold. We must first raise the consciousness of our black men and women in law enforcement, challenging them to stand up for justice for our people and stop placing a meager police salary over the lives and welfare of our black brothers and sisters. Black cops also need to understand that black lives matter! Until we, as African Americans, accept this truth as more than a slogan, we will continue to see varying instances where we devalue ourselves for the enrichment and perpetuation of institutions that are the architects and the gatekeepers of our own oppression. Next, we should demand criminal accountability for all of those involved in the violation of the rights of African Americans, whether those cops be black or white. This would be a start in attacking the culture of silence within police departments that protects the guilty at the expense of and justice for the victims.

K. Gerald Torrence

The (Not So) Curious Case of Sandra Bland

Originally posted August 9, 2015

The peculiar circumstances surrounding the death of Sandra Bland while in the custody of the Waller County, Texas, jail continue to become more and more troubling. The case of the African American female who was found hanged in her jail cell three days after being arrested for failing to signal a lane change should shock the conscious of any person with an ounce of humanity or sense of justice. To be pulled over by law enforcement for an alleged traffic violation and end up hanging dead from a trash bag in a jail cell brings into focus the very real hazards of "driving while black" in America. It's difficult, if not impossible, to imagine such a scenario developing under similar circumstances involving a white woman.

The facts surrounding Ms. Bland's death raise numerous questions regarding the police officer's conduct and her treatment at the Waller County jail:

1. Why was she arrested for failing to put out a cigarette?
2. Why did the take down and handcuffing of Bland take place off-camera?
3. Why was she still in jail three days after her arrest?
4. Why was a large trash bag strong enough to support her body in her jail cell?
5. Why was Bland not closely monitored after allegedly indicating previous bouts of depression and suicidal thoughts?

Sandra Bland's untimely and needless death, which smacks of murder, gives poetic resonance to the reality of what African American's feel and live with on a daily basis. At the risk of stating the obvious, black people throughout the history of America have been constantly reminded of the racial disparity in every phase of the American criminal justice system. From disproportionate traffic stops, arrests, convictions, and sentencings to untimely deaths at the hands of white police officers, it has been historically and statistically proven that black lives and freedom are worth far less than that of white folk. The current mantra recently adopted by white politicians like Hillary Clinton and others that "Black Lives Matter" is in and of itself an indictment of the American criminal justice system, which results in the overwhelmingly disproportionate killing and incarceration of African Americans at the hands of police, prosecutors, and judges.

Justice Taney articulated the legal and social reality that the Negro had "no rights which the white man was bound to respect."

The very statement that black lives matter underscores the absurdity of the question implicit in the statement. By even having to say it, we call into question the value and relative worth of African American life here in the United States. Black lives have never mattered with respect to the relative and comparable worth of white people; they mattered only with regard to the loss of property and free or cheap labor. The devaluation of black lives is rooted and steeped in history, where in the U.S. Constitution, the Negro is only referenced as property measuring 3/5 of a person. The relative worthlessness of black life and liberty is further reinforced in early Supreme Court cases such as Scott v. Sanford (1857), wherein Justice Taney articulated the legal and social reality that the Negro had "no rights which the white man was bound to respect." This historical pronouncement had grave social and political implications for the Negro at the time it was made and still reverberates through the consciousness of every white person and every institution, and undergirds a system of government and laws that dispense justice and opportunity in a way that is fundamentally separate and unequal.

With the advent and increasing use of police body cameras, cell phone video recording, and other modern technologies, the viewing public has become increasingly aware of the almost daily incidents of murder and injustice against African Americans that heretofore went unnoticed, undocumented, and unprosecuted. The harsh realities and dangers of being black in America are now on display for the world to see and can no longer be hidden by police cover-ups and political sleight of hand. Do we really need more investigations and statistics to corroborate the continuing disregard of black life at the hands of law enforcement? The tragic case of Sandra Bland is neither new nor novel in the centuries-old institutionalized devaluation of black life and liberty in America. Unfortunately, it is only one of the more recent examples that have shockingly come to light. The evidence is clear, convincing, and unmitigated. In the United States of America, black lives have never mattered to the extent and relative comparison to those of whites. The only legitimate question that continues to go unanswered is: What is America willing to do about it?

What is it about whiteness that makes it so desirable?

W.E.B. DuBois

BACK TO BLACK

K. Gerald Torrence

Back to Black

Originally posted April 16, 2015

If there were ever a clarion call for African American college-bound students to reconsider their increasing predilection to choose white universities as their preference for higher education, it is now. The recent flurry of high-profile incidents of racism expose the underlying racist undercurrent and hostility toward African American students at white institutions of higher learning.

The noose hanging incident—where a hangman's noose was conspicuously placed in a common area—at Duke University only days before winning the NCAA men's basketball championship underscores the discrimination that black students and faculty endure on a regular basis at white colleges across this country. Shamefully, but not shockingly, the noose incident at Duke University is only one of several examples of blatant acts of racism, including hateful speech occurring on the Duke campus and directed at black students. In an MSNBC interview, a leading African American student at Duke profoundly stated the realities of black college life at white universities when he said that, "the occasional display of public demonstrations of racism doesn't bother me. What's most concerning is the daily acts of racism that black students contend with every day." A female African American student at Duke was quoted as saying, "punishing the culprit will not change the culture of racism on campus." She added that friends of hers also experienced racism at Duke.

The noose hanging from a tree outside the student center is only the latest reincarnation of a centuries-old symbol used to terrorize and intimidate black people by the Ku Klux Klan, other white supremacist groups, and individuals seeking to deny equality to blacks. The fact that this potent symbol of racism and white supremacy is being openly flaunted on college campuses more than fifty years after the Supreme Court case, *Brown v. Board of Education of Topeka,* speaks volumes as to the continuing resistance to black acceptance on white college campuses. Although the Brown case outlawed the doctrine of "separate but equal" and opened the door to integration in schools previously denying entrance to black students like Ole Miss, University of Alabama, and others, it's impossible to legislate morality and civility. The underlying culture of white supremacy and black inferiority is too deeply ingrained in the social and political fabric of this country. The United States of America was constructed with the building blocks of separate and unequal. Racism is in its DNA. Forced integration has not, and will never change, the hearts and minds of those whose birth right and promise of prosperity rests on the bedrock principles of European dominance and control.

The recent racist video chant at the University of Oklahoma by members of the white fraternity Sigma Alpha Epsilon is another example of the volcanic eruption of racism at white colleges across America. The chant, "There will never be a nigger at SAE … You can hang them from a tree, but they will never sign with me … There will never be a nigger at SAE," illustrates, I believe, the true sentiments of most whites with regard to black integration into white colleges and universities. These institutions are the bastions and gatekeepers of Anglo/European culture and white supremacy. The condemnation of the video by OU President David Boren and head football coach Bob Stoops was predictable and more than a little contrived. Their feigned outrage begs the question of motivation and is consistent with this modern age of political correctness. After all, what could they say? Other than to condemn the racist acts as an anomaly and not representative of the University as whole, there was no other viable response. Shortly after the incident became public, head coach Bob Stoops participated in a protest and "walk out" along with black OU football players and supporters. Stoops, of course, is no dummy. He realizes that his livelihood and the millions of NCAA dollars that flow into the OU campus coffers rest on the contentment and participation of the black athletes who comprise a visible majority of OU's, and other major college football powerhouses, starting lineup.

In these modern, ultra-competitive times, major sports programs can't compete at the elite levels without the black athlete. They've tried and failed. Former University of Alabama football coach Paul "Bear" Bryant fielded mostly all-white teams until the very end of his career. Bryant finally capitulated after other white universities began to saturate their teams with black players, resulting in a competitive advantage. Bryant then employed the old adage, "if you can't beat them, join them."

Those same institutions that once vowed never to integrate ... tolerate the average black student non-athlete as a necessary evil.

Wow! What a difference a few decades make. I can remember sitting in front of the television set as a small boy with my father and asking, "Daddy, who are you pulling for?" My father's answer would invariably be, "I don't know, chief, which team has a colored boy?" It's amazing how far we have come in the way of integrated college athletics, where now, in the two major market sports of football and basketball, you are hard-pressed to find a white player on the starting lineup. All the star players are black, and all of the coaches and athletic directors are white, with very few exceptions. Yet, what seems like a windfall for black athletes has actually been a financial windfall for white colleges and universities. Those same institutions that once vowed never to integrate have changed their tune and now openly court black athletes and tolerate the average non-athlete black student as a necessary evil.

One of the biggest lies, myths, and preconceived notions about modern-day big time college athletics is that in order to be drafted, you must attend one of the big-name white universities. This is historically untrue and a new-age variation of "the white man's ice is colder" syndrome. Black players were going into the pros in the 1950s, 60s, and 70s from black colleges like Tennessee State, Florida A&M, Grambling, Bethune-Cookman, Southern University, and Texas Southern—long before integration took hold as inevitable and acceptable on white college campuses. Then, just like now, if you had the talent, white professional scouts would find you.

So, the question of whether it's necessary for black students and athletes to suffer the humiliation and degradation of racism and disparate treatment in order to reach their goals of success at the professional levels and beyond academia can be answered unequivocally. History shows us that the answer is "No." We don't have to be validated by involvement at white institutions to prove our worth. We never did. Black overachievers from HBCUs have been making their mark on society for over 150 years. The tragedy is that many of these successes have gone unrecorded and, therefore, unnoticed. Let us not be fooled. The oppressor has always sought to hide our greatness and take credit for our accomplishments. If it was good enough for my father and mother, it's good enough for me.

At one time, it was useful and necessary to break down barriers of legal and social discrimination. That time served African Americans very well. Now is the time to return home to our roots and strengthen by our attendance and patronage the nurturing hand of black colleges, which gave the Negro race its first opportunity for higher education. When all of the other doors were closed for our educational advancement due to racism and Jim Crow, we built our own, and we educated our own. In many ways, integration was the death knell for the celebration of the spirit of black, educational, and entrepreneurial independence and excellence. We have truly lost our way.

K. Gerald Torrence

"Back to Black" must become more than just a slogan but a mantra that symbolizes and mobilizes a return to our rich heritage ...

Even though the University of Oklahoma expelled two students for leading a racist song that sparked outrage across the country when it became public, that action by the university doesn't solve the problem of racism on American college campuses. The underlying problem is systemic and endemic. Racism and white supremacy is ingrained in the social, economic, and political fabric of these institutions, which were built on the backs of blacks but not for their education or inclusion.

So, while universities and the national media will try to paint the picture of acts like these being isolated incidents, common sense and high-profile examples of racism in all facets of American life tell us it's not. My question is: Why? Are we blacks gluttons for punishment or just so enamored with the prospects of assimilation with white folk that we willingly suffer the slings and arrows of demoralizing abuse and disparate treatment? I again ask the question first raised by W.E.B. DuBois, "What is it about whiteness that makes it so desirable?" Surely, in 2015, African Americans must realize that there is nothing inherently magical about being white and nothing inherently inferior about being black. We have the ability to create our own institutions and traditions of excellence, just like our ancestors. "Back to Black" must become more than just a slogan but a mantra that symbolizes and mobilizes a return to our rich heritage and legacies which produced many of the great African Americans of the last century.

Real diversity can only come through genuine acceptance ... cultural appreciation for that which has forever been viewed as inferior among Europeans.

I suggest that the solution is not to try to change white folk's opinion of us or demonstrate that we are just as competent and talented as them. We've done that for centuries, and it has not made us any more acceptable as a race in any significant way. What we need is a return to our historically black colleges and universities in numbers and patronage, which equals our mass exodus over the last forty years to the universities of the empire. We must return back to black colleges where we are not marginalized, tolerated, or stereotyped, all in the name of diversity, which in reality is a concept that is unattainable aside from numbers and quotas on a spreadsheet. Real diversity can only come through genuine acceptance, shared respect, and cultural appreciation for that which has forever been viewed as inferior among Europeans.

With respect to the African American Oklahoma football recruit who decided against attending OU after the racist video rant came to light, I applaud his decision. A message must be sent! I caution the young man, however, against substituting one racist institution for another. All white colleges and universities contain racist elements and attitudes which will not go away in our lifetimes, if ever. Why not return to our black colleges, the only safe haven against the spoken and unspoken anti-black sentiments which undergird the very fabric of this country. I say, "Back to Black," young African American man and woman. Let's rebuild and re-establish the proud legacies of our own historically black colleges and universities before it's too late. Our schools are under attack just like our young black men and the civil rights gains of the last fifty years. We must make "Back to Black" more than a slogan. We must make it a movement.

K. Gerald Torrence

The New Black Power

Originally posted December 7, 2015

At long last, the sleeping giant which lay dormant on white college campuses has been awakened. The raw power which was demonstrated on the national stage by the University of Missouri football team and the organized efforts of black student organizations recently caught an entire nation by surprise. If a strike or boycott by black football players can force a domino effect of resignations by the University President and the Chancellor of the University of Missouri System campuses, is the status quo of systemic racism safe at any predominantly white institutions (PWIs) in America? This certainly must be a question raised and pondered in the minds of many in light of the chain of events leading to the dramatic fall of the Universities of Missouri's top officials. In retrospect, the accomplishment of the united front of black students, faculty, and athletes to spawn historic change is nothing short of amazing. This non-violent black solidarity movement, unprecedented in both impact and effect, could represent the new evolution of black activism through the flexing of economic muscle.

The reverberations of this take down will rumble across white colleges and universities for years to come. In the twinkling of an eye, the black students, athletes, and faculty stopped waiting for change and forced it through the only method that power and institutional racism will yield to: the power of the dollar bill. This economic juggernaut, wielded by the University of Missouri black football players and held by black students at all PWIs in America, will be daunting and unstoppable if it is only put to use.

The University of Missouri, like most major college football programs, relies on a vast majority of black athletes to fuel their multi-million dollar programs run by multi-millionaire coaches, the vast majority of whom are white. According to a 2010 report of the NCAA, 45.8% of Division I football players were black.[13] At the University of Missouri, out of 84 full scholarships awarded to the football team, 58 go to black athletes.[14] Between 2007 and 2010, black men were 2.8% of full-time, degree-seeking undergraduate students, but 57.1% of football teams and 64.3% of basketball teams. This statistic is all the more telling and ironic considering that traditional powerhouse and 16- time national champion University of Alabama did not have any black players until 1971 but now fields a team that is exclusively dominated by black players.

You begin to see the picture of an existence that is not far removed from the experiences of the first black students to cross the color line back in the 1960s.

This overwhelming majority of African American players who fill the rosters of NCAA football (and basketball) programs represents an untapped source of leverage and power, heretofore unrealized, that can effectuate social justice and racial equality. In stark contrast to the majority of white student athletes, however, these same black players oftentimes struggle financially to afford the basic necessities and creature comforts that most white students take for granted. On top of this inequity, black athletes and students are often marginalized, ostracized, and forced to exist in racist environments that segregate and exclude them at every turn. Add to this the indignities of racial slurs and threats of bodily harm that are routine at white colleges, and you begin to see the picture of an existence that is not far removed from the experiences of the first black students to cross the color line back in the 1960s.

The power exhibited by black students and athletes at the University of Missouri, however, is a potential game changer. The genie is now out of the bottle, never to be called back into the cozy confines of the status quo. Make no mistake, the decision by University President Timothy Wolfe to resign was not a moral one. Wolfe's decision to resign had little to do with, as he put it, "something [that] needed to be done that was immediate and substantial for us to heal" and more about the loss of revenue—Missouri would have had to pay a million dollar fine if the football team had failed to play its next scheduled game against Brigham Young University (BYU).

The dissatisfaction with University leadership had been brewing for months. A series of racist incidents that had been brought to Wolfe's attention were essentially ignored or glossed over in the minds of black student organization leaders and black faculty. Missouri Students Association black president Payton Head sparked the debate of racial intolerance in September 2015 when he posted on Facebook about an incident in which he was the target of racial epithets. According to Head, these types of incidents at the University "were not uncommon."

In October 2015, a white student interrupted a homecoming event by the Legion of Black Collegians and used racial slurs against the participants. As reported by *The New York Times*, the incident was dismissed by Wolfe after black students brought it to his attention. After a swastika scrawled in feces was found on campus later that month, the activist group Concerned Student 1950 was formed—signifying the year the first black student was admitted to the University. The organization then began to pick up momentum as they demanded that Wolfe address the issues of rampant racism on campus.[15] In hindsight, Wolfe ignored the students' demands at his own peril.

After essentially ignoring the black students' demands for his resignation for months, the swiftness of Wolfe's departure once the football team threatened boycott was startling. As reported by *The New York Times*, "the African American football players of the University of Missouri tweeted that they were going on strike until President

Tim Wolfe resigns or is removed."[16] Approximately 36 hours after the threat of economic sanctions by the football team, not only had Wolfe resigned, but University of Missouri System Chancellor R. Bowen Loftin also agreed to resign effective at the end of the year. Clearly, it was the football players' threat, which potentially could have cost the school millions of dollars, that was the catalyst for the change of strategy by the University and the System's Board of Curators.

Imagine if similar strategies to combat racism and effectuate structural policy change were adopted by united black athletes at predominantly white schools across the country. Perhaps a new era of dialogue about inclusiveness and tolerance might sweep across white colleges and universities ushered in by this new black militancy. On the other hand, maybe the continuing struggle for equality at PWIs might facilitate a reverse exodus of our elite black athletes back to historically black colleges and universities (HBCUs), thereby raising their profiles and economic status commensurate with the millions of dollars and publicity they generate for white institutions.

Surely, history will judge this moment to be revolutionary in the centuries' old continuing struggle against institutional racism and the scourge of white supremacy.

To call this demonstration of black power by the University of Missouri students a watershed moment in the history of sports and higher education in this country does not overstate its impact. Surely, history will judge this moment to be revolutionary in the centuries' old continuing struggle against institutional racism and the scourge of white supremacy.

References

[1] Carson, E. Ann. "Prisoners in 2014." *Bureau of Justice Statistics*. U.S. Department of Justice, September 2015. <http://www.bjs.gov/content/pub/pdf/p14.pdf>.

[2] Ibid.

[3] Perez, Evan. "Justice Report Finds Systematic Discrimination Against African- Americans in Ferguson." *CNN.com*. Turner Broadcasting System, Inc., 4 March 2015. <http://www.cnn.com/2015/03/03/politics/justice-report- ferguson-discrimination/index.html>.

[4] Ibid.

[5] Carson, E. Ann. "Prisoners in 2014." *Bureau of Justice Statistics*. U.S. Department of Justice, September 2015. <http://www.bjs.gov/content/pub/pdf/p14.pdf>.

[6] Palazzolo, Joe. "For Americans Who Served Time, Landing a Job Proves Tricky."

The Wall Street Journal. Dow Jones & Company, Inc., 17 May 2015.

[7] Ibid.

[8] Carson, E. Ann. "Prisoners in 2014." *Bureau of Justice Statistics*. U.S. Department of Justice, September 2015. <http://www.bjs.gov/content/pub/pdf/p14.pdf>.

[9] Coates, Ta Nehisi. "The Black Family in the Age of Mass Incarceration."

The Atlantic. The Atlantic Monthly Group, October 2015.

[10] Ibid.

[11] Will, George. "Black Single Mothers Are Biggest Impediment to Progress."

The Huffington Post. TheHuffingtonPost.com, Inc., 26 August 2013.

[12] Baptist, Edward E. *The Half Has Never Been Told: Slavery and the Making of American Capitalism*. New York: Basic Books, 2014.

[13] "Blacks Now a Majority On Football Teams." *ESPN.com*. ESPN Inc., 8 December 2010. <http://espn.go.com/espn/print?id=5901855>.

[14] Belkin, Douglas, and Melissa Korn. "Student Protests Trigger Resignations at Missouri." *The Wall Street Journal*. Dow Jones & Company, Inc., 10 November 2015.

[15] Eligon, John, and Richard Pérez-Peña. "University of Missouri Protests Spur a Day of Change." *The New York Times*. Arthur Ochs Sulzberger, Jr., 9 November 2015.

[16] Nocera, Joe. "College Athletes' Potential Realized in Missouri Resignations."

The New York Times. Arthur Ochs Sulzberger, Jr., 10 November 2015.

Index

"Kerner Report", 30
"The Negro Family"
    report on, 31, 32
"The Rising" (Vesey, Denmark), 52

16th Street Baptist Church
    (Birmingham), 52

African Americans
    citizenship of, 10, 28, 46, 72
    incarceration of, 10, 23, 29, 30, 68, 79, 92
Angelou, Maya, 57

back to black, more than a
    slogan, 86, 87
Baltimore (Maryland)
    culture of racism in, 82,
Baptist, Edward, 93
    black and brown (people of color), 11, 26, 37, 65
black lives matter, 51, 77, 79
Bland, Sandra
    death of, 41, 43, 71
Boren, David, 83

Brown v. Board, 9, 45, 47, 71, 83
Brown, Michael
    death of, 41, 43, 71, 78
Brown, Morris Reverend, 52
Bryant, Paul "Bear", 84

Central High School (Little Rock), 45
Charleston (South Carolina)
    massacre in, 51
    slave revolt in, 52
Civil Rights Act
    of 1864, 22
    of 1964, 22, 59,
Civil Rights Movement, 43, 52
Civil War (American), 9, 38, 40, 54
CNN, 20, 60, 92
Constitution (U.S.), 4, 10, 69, 72, 79, 49, 73, 79, 88
Cosby, Bill, 57–58
criminal justice system, 9, 16, 28, 68, 79
Dent, Richard, 19
Dred Scott, 23

driving while black, 78
DuBois, W.E.B., 71, 86
Emancipation Proclamation, 9, 22, 38, 47, 71
Emmanuel A.M.E. Church (Charleston), 51, 52
empire (American), 52, 66, 67, 68, 74, 76
Exodus: Gods and Kings (film), 62
Ferguson (Missouri)
   culture of racism in, 20, 37, 73,
Garner, Eric
   death of, 66, 71
Gilliam, Joe, 19
Goodell, Roger, 15, 16, 19
Graham, Toya, 67
Gray, Freddie
   death of, 67, 66
HBCUs, 19, 44, 85, 91,
   Bethune-Cookman University, 85
   Florida A&M University, 85
   Grambling State University, 19, 85
   Southern University, 19, 85
   Tennessee State University, 19, 85
   Texas Southern University, 85
Hogan, Larry (Governor), 66
Holy Bible, 63
   characters of, 63, 74

   quotes from, 15, 25, 63
Humphrey, Claude, 19
Jim Crow, 9, 40, 43, 44, 46, 49, 66, 85
King, Martin Luther, Jr., 32, 43, 47, 52, 57
Ku Klux Klan (KKK), 40, 54, 83
Loftin, R. Bowen, 91
Malcolm X, 43, 57
mass exodus
to white colleges and universities, 19, 83
media personalities
Lemon, Don, 61
Limbaugh, Rush, 3, 41
Sharpton, Al, 60
MSNBC, 82
Murdoch, Rupert, 62–63
National Guard
intervention by, 45,
NBA
racist heritage, 19
response to racism, 6–7, 8
NCAA
News Corporation, 62
NFL
racist heritage, 19
Obama, Barack (President)
and acknowledgement of racism, 52
and anti-black sentiment, 3, 38, 40, 87

and Nobel Peace Prize, 35
and Western Imperialism, 35–37
Peterson, Adrian, 14, 16, 19, 67
Pinckney, Clementa (State Senator), 51
   police brutality
culture of, 22, 27, 50, 75
predominantly white institutions, 88
racial divide, 31, 59
institutional, 2, 14, 88, 91
media influence on, 19, 65, 66, 75, 80, 97
on white college campuses, 21, 51, 93, 94, 96, 99–102, 100
scourge of, 7, 43, 91
structural, 11, 14, 20, 38, 46, 72
Rawlings-Blake, Stephanie (Mayor), 66
Reconstruction, 38, 40, 41, 46, 54, 68
Rice, Ray, 16, 19
Roof, Dylann, 51, 52
Sherman, William T. (General), 39
Silver, Adam, 6, 7
Special Field Order 15, 39
Sterling, Donald, 2, 3, 4, 5, 7, 19, 22, 72
Stoops, Bob, 83
Taney, Roger B. (Justice), 19, 23, 69
The Half Has Never Been Told, 39
   transatlantic slave trade, 14, 47

U.S. Justice Department
   and exposing racism, 19
U.S. Presidents
   impact on racism, 33, 34, 43, 44
U.S. Supreme Court
   and anti-black sentiment, 21, 88
Uncle Tom, 19, 68, 83
Vesey, Denmark, 52
Voting Rights Act, 59
Wallace, George (Governor), 19
Washington, Booker T., 71
white supremacy, 2, 9, 11, 38, 42, 45, 46, 49, 50, 63, 66, 72, 73, 83
   culture of, 25, 30, 57, 94
groups supporting, 54
Wolfe, Timothy, 90, 91
Woodson, Carter G., 46

About the Author

K. Gerald Torrence

Gerald Torrence is a lawyer, educator, writer, and social activist living in Atlanta, Georgia. Having grown up in a family of lifelong educators, he understands the importance of information and education in raising the consciousness and improving the upward mobility of oppressed peoples. He received his undergraduate degree at Morehouse College and his juris doctorate from the University of Arkansas at Little Rock. After practicing law for nineteen years, he returned to academia and spent over ten years as an assistant professor teaching business law at Tuskegee University, Morehouse College, Philander Smith College, and Arkansas Baptist College.

Torrence is the owner and founder of The Truth Teller Enterprises, a platform for social justice, political activism, and cultural consciousness. His writings have been published in the *Denver Urban Spectrum* and Atlanta-area publications. He is also an ordained Baptist minister.

Torrence blogs at www.the-truth-teller.com.

www.ingramcontent.com/pod-product-compliance
Lightning Source LLC
Chambersburg PA
CBHW052033030426
42337CB00027B/4981